Lady Nithsdale and the Jacobites

CW01663786

Lady Nithsdale and the Jacobites

Flora Maxwell Stuart

Traquair House
Innerleithen
Peeblesshire
EH44 6PW

In Memory of my husband Peter Maxwell Stuart
20th Laird of Traquair

© Flora Maxwell Stuart 1995
First published 1995

ISBN 0 9504424 1 0

Acknowledgements

First of all I would like to offer my gratitude to Her Majesty the Queen for her gracious permission to use material from the Stuart Papers at Windsor.

I would also like to offer my most sincere thanks to the many people who have helped me over the long period of time that it has taken to complete this book and I regret that I am unable to mention them all by name. Particular gratitude is due to Professor R.M. Mitchison who was good enough to read the manuscript and to make constructive comments, to Mother Prioress and the nuns in the English Convent in Bruges who kindly showed me their treasures and supplied photographs, the Earl of Powis for information on the Herbert family, Major Williams for checking the relevant pages, and Nancy Pearson for giving me information about Clementina Sobieska gained from her research in Italian Archives. I am most grateful to Dr E. T. Corp and the Musée des Antiquités Nationales, St Germain-en-Laye, Mr Alistair Cherry and the Trustees of the National Library of Scotland, the Drambuie Collection, the National Galleries of Scotland, the Scottish Tourist Board, the National Museums of Scotland, Jarrolds of Norwich, Messrs Woodmansterne, the Courtauld Institute of Art, Country Life Picture Library, and the Powis Collection, Powis Castle (The National Trust) for kindly supplying me with photographs. Also to Alasdair MacFarlane and Simon Scott Moncrieff for photographing portraits and objects in Traquair House and Brian Vaughan for his drawing of the Muti Palace.

FLORA MAXWELL STUART OF TRAQUAIR 1995.

Front cover illustration: Lady Nithsdale by John Medina, Traquair House

Designed by George Bowie, HMSO and printed in Scotland for HMSO

Contents

Powis Castle exterior, Powis Castle, (The National Trust). Photograph: Country Life picture library.

CHAPTER 1

Childhood

Popery is such a thing as cannot, but for want of a word to express it, be called a religion.
ANDREW MARVELL

On a dark February afternoon, Lord Nithsdale sat in his cell in the Tower of London. Resigned to death, he was composing the speech that he intended to give from the scaffold, before he was beheaded the following morning. For extra security he had been put under lock and key in the Lieutenant's Lodgings, two storeys up and a drop of forty feet from his small, barred window to the ground below. A warder, armed with halberd, stood at his door and guards were on duty in the Council Chamber outside, and at the main entrance. The whole Tower was on the alert, for they knew that they had important prisoners in their care. George I wished to make an example of the "Jacobite lords" so they would cause him no more trouble in the future. Yet, within a few hours, through the courage and ingenuity of his wife, Lord Nithsdale was set free. With great daring Winifred Nithsdale managed to save her husband from his fate.

Winifred Herbert came from the marriage of two important Welsh landowning families. Her mother was Elizabeth Somerset, daughter of the Marquess of Worcester and her father was William Herbert, the 2nd Marquess and 3rd Baron Powis. Winifred, born in 1672, was the youngest of their six children. Her eldest sister Mary was then thirteen and Lucy, the fifth child, was four, with her brother William and her sisters Frances and Anne spaced out in between.

The young family grew up within the massive walls of Powis Castle which stood majestically on a platform of rock over looking the Severn Valley in mid-Wales, and in the family house in London. Descended from a younger branch of the Earls of Pembroke, Sir Edward Herbert had purchased Powis Castle a hundred years previously and had adapted it then to an Elizabethan way of life. During the Civil War, the 1st Baron Powis had made a courageous effort to defend the castle from Cromwell's troops but, after one gateway had been completely destroyed, the rest of the building received such a battering that he was forced to surrender. Later, under Charles II, his loyalty was rewarded and he had been created the 1st Earl of Powis.

To celebrate this honour and to herald the years of peace which it was hoped had arrived with the return of the monarchy, he had set to work to rebuild his castle, employing the architect William Winde to add further improvements. In case the king

Powis Castle Grand Stair, Powis Castle, (The National Trust).

might care to visit him, he had tactfully added a magnificent state bedroom: furnished with a vast bed raised on an altar-like platform, it was worthy of any monarch who believed in a divine right to rule. The former narrow stair was replaced with a grand one of oak and the Italian painter Verrio was commissioned to decorate the ceiling above. A library was also created and filled with a wide range of books, so that the building gradually lost its role as a fortress and became instead a great country house.

Accounts of the time give an idea of the life that was led in the castle where, as the seasons followed each other, the land and sea offered up a fresh harvest and each month required a new labour. In January bundles of feathers, hops and "tickers" were used for making bolsters. Fish was plentiful in March, red and white herrings were ordered, mussels in their hundreds, as well as "28 trouts". In April a calf was fat enough to be killed and hay and oats were bought in for the horses. Sixpence was paid for five quarts of mustard seed in May, 120 eggs were bought and a delivery of sand meant the annual scouring of pots and pans. Strawberries were picked in June and, in this month too, wick "yearn" was obtained for the making of candles. In July vinegar was prepared ready for autumn preserving. In August, honey was taken from the bees and it was the time for flowers and herbs to be gathered. Jane Cooper and Betty Cowdal were paid four pence a quart for violets, two pence a quart for cowslips and eight pence for a basket of wood sorrel. Mushrooms were gathered in late summer and plums and apples picked as they ripened. Oysters abounded in October and were carried to the castle in their hundreds to be eaten fresh, or pickled for the winter months. Finally, at the end of the year, twenty-two woodcock and a dozen newts' tongues were sent down to London.

It was a regular and secure existence; or so it might have seemed to a child. And of the masses said in secret, the ever looming danger of belonging to a proscribed religion, the vacillating policy of the king, Winifred would have known nothing. For the Herberts had kept faith with the Roman Catholic religion and so were technically subject to the severe penal laws of the time. These laws stated that those who did not attend the services of the Anglican Church once a week, or who did not take communion three times a year, were guilty of "recusancy" and required them to pay a fine of £20 a month or two-thirds of their income, whichever the government preferred. It was a felony to attend mass and a serious offence to be found in possession of any article of devotion. Catholic priests or those who sheltered them were liable to be punished by being sentenced to death. Catholics were also precluded from holding any kind of public office, the universities, the law and the services, by the necessity of taking an oath of allegiance which acknowledged the king as head of the Church, free from the jurisdiction of the Pope.

Yet, devastating as these laws might be, under Charles II their enforcement had become lax and there were many ways for the rich to avoid paying their fines. Lord Powis was still able to take his seat in the House of Lords and it does not seem that his vast estates in Wales, Ireland and England had been noticeably diminished. Catholicism still lingered within the royal family. Queen Catherine of Braganza, like her mother-in-law the French Henrietta Maria, was a Roman Catholic. She had been allowed to have a Catholic chapel in St James's Palace and even for a time housed a convent of nuns there. Young priests, trained by the Jesuits on the Continent, returned freely to Britain where they took up positions in country houses and were rarely apprehended.

However, when rumours began to circulate that the king's brother, James, the Duke of York, had converted to Catholicism, the government took action. In 1673 the Test Act was introduced which obliged all office-holders and all ranks of the services to declare their disbelief in the doctrine of substantiation, to produce a certificate that they had recently taken Anglican Communion and to take the oaths of Allegiance and Supremacy in open court.

The rumours proved to be well founded, and when James, an extremely able Lord High Admiral, openly admitted his conversion to Roman Catholicism, he was forced to resign. James's religion was of the utmost importance, for Charles II had no legitimate children and his brother was his heir to the throne. James had two Protestant daughters Mary and Anne whose mother Anne Hyde had died, but the following year he disturbed the public still further by taking a second wife, the fifteen-year-old Catholic, Mary Beatrice of Modena. Should this young wife produce a son, the child would take precedence over his half-sisters and Britain would be subject to a Catholic king.

A fear of Catholics had been festering beneath the surface for years. Catholics were considered to be sinister beings with their masses and weird beliefs, controlled from abroad by a foreign Pope. It was thought that they had been responsible for the fire of London as well as all kinds of natural disasters and when it was further discovered that the king himself had been involved in secret negotiations with his Catholic cousin, King Louis of France, it was the final straw. The people were filled with fear and outrage, and a deranged ex-seminarian named Titus Oates allowed the dam of pent-up fury to burst.

This young man announced that he had discovered a plot between the Pope, the Jesuits and the British Catholics whereby they would assassinate the king, exterminate the government and replace it with one of their own: his words, reflecting as they did what many had suspected for some time, were instantly believed. A state of emergency was declared as he daily revealed further developments of the plot. Lord Powis, he claimed, was to be Lord High Treasurer in the new Catholic government and, together with Lord Petre, had supposedly agreed to raise an army in Wales where he would be joined by Spanish troops.

The country was overtaken by hysteria. Overnight Lord Powis and anyone named by Titus Oates was thrown into the Tower and Catholic houses all over Britain were repeatedly searched. Large rewards encouraged informers and even the good Protestant Samuel Pepys spent some weeks in the Tower on the evidence of an unfaithful servant.

As hundreds of laymen and priests were imprisoned, Charles realised that the government was watching him closely and that he was powerless to intervene. He found himself signing the death warrants of men he knew to be innocent but calculated coolly that such frenzy could not last and would gradually burn itself out. The king prudently dispatched his brother James and his young wife, first abroad and then to Scotland, but they were not allowed to take their young daughters with them and, during their absence, five-year-old Isabella died.

Lady Powis by John Michael Wright, Powis Collection, Powis Castle, (The National Trust).
Photograph: Courtauld Institute of Art.

Meanwhile, Lady Powis, an impetuous and fearless woman, soon joined her husband in the Tower. She had joined a charitable group who visited the Catholic prisoners and helped them by tracing witnesses to speak for them at their trials. One of the prisoners was the Venerable Oliver Plunkett, an Irish priest who met his death and was later beatified, who wrote: "The English Catholics here were most charitable to me, and in my trial did all for me that even my brother would do. They are rare Catholics".

Before long Lady Powis was approached by a young man of dubious reputation, aptly named Dangerfield, who asked whether he might be allowed to help. To this she rashly agreed, but realising what generous rewards were being handed out to informers, the young criminal then maintained that he had found incriminating papers, hidden in a tub of meal which implicated her group in a plot to kill the king. As usual he was believed and Lady Powis and her associates were all taken into custody.

With the exception of Lord Stafford, who was tried and executed, the remainder of the Catholic lords were never brought to trial. As the king had predicted, the country did gradually grow tired of witch-hunting and the discovery of the Rye House Plot, a Whig conspiracy to murder both the king and the Duke of York, brought a surge of loyalty towards the two Stuart brothers. Lady Powis had already returned to her family when the duke was allowed back from Scotland and James immediately made it his business to secure the release of Lord Powis. A few months later the House of Lords duly cancelled his impeachment.

Lord Powis had spent four years in the Tower but during that time improvements continued at the Castle. After his release both he and his wife spent less time at Whitehall and more at St James's Palace with the Duke and Duches of York, to whom they became very close. Only two years later the fifty-five-year-old King Charles was struck down by a stroke, and within a few days, his life came to an end. As he lay dying he was converted to Roman Catholicism by Father Huddleston, a priest brought to his bedside by his brother, James.

CHAPTER 2

James II

On a fine spring day in April 1685 the streets of London thronged with an excited crowd. James II had chosen St George's Day for his coronation and his people were out to enjoy themselves. It was many years since a queen had been crowned. The Catholic Catherine of Braganza, the previous queen, and Henrietta Maria, wife of Charles I, had refused to take part in the ceremony. But their co-religionist James had taken one of the few astute actions of his reign and had altered the service so that it could cause no offence either to himself or to anyone else. His beautiful dark-haired queen, still only twenty-seven years of age, gave an added glamour to the occasion. She had increased her popularity further by paying off the debts of eighty small debtors and thus releasing them from prison.

Between Westminster Hall and the Abbey, the street had been covered with a blue carpet, and scaffolding had been erected so that as many people as possible could witness the procession. The appearance of the hereditary herb women was a sign that the proceedings were about to start. Dressed in tight bodices and looped up skirts they carried baskets of spring flowers and sweet smelling herbs, which they scattered in readiness for the royal procession. They were followed by drums, trumpets, scarlet clothed dignitaries and the queen who, composed and dignified as she advanced under a canopy of gold cloth, "shone like an angel" in a dress of white and silver embroidered brocade, heavily encrusted with diamonds. Among the unmarried daughters of earls who bore the magnificent silk train edged with gold lace and lined with ermine was Anne Herbert. Her brother William acted as page to the king and Lord and Lady Powis stood among the peers and peeresses in their crimson robes. At 3 p.m. the king was crowned and a shout went up from the congregation. The lords and ladies placed their coronets upon their heads and guns could be heard firing from the Tower and in St James's Park. The queen's new crown had especially been made for her and was covered with so many precious stones that the gold could not be seen, but the king made do with the crown that had been made for his brother Charles. A little too large for him, it sat unsteadily upon his head, as the superstitious were quick to notice.

As the procession re-formed to make its way out of the Abbey, Queen Mary Beatrice exchanged a few words with the king's daughter, Princess Anne, who sat with her husband the Prince of Denmark in a box which had been specially constructed for

James II by Sir Peter Lely (National Galleries of Scotland).

them. Then, to the sound of Purcell's triumphant music, the whole congregation followed their new monarch out into Westminster Hall where a vast banquet lay waiting. That night fireworks were let off, lighting up the Thames in bursts of colour, and a great fountain of wine was set up to celebrate the day.

England once again had a Catholic king and James was determined to introduce the principle of religious toleration as soon as possible. It was not long before Lord Powis was created a marquess and admitted to the Privy Council while Lady Powis became one of the queen's closest companions. They brought their family from their castle in

Mary Beatrice of Modena, William Wissing (National Galleries of Scotland).

Wales and rebuilt their house in Lincoln's Inn Fields which had been vandalised by the mob in the time of Titus Oates. A water cistern was constructed on the roof where, for the amusement of the two youngest daughters Winifred and Lucy, goldfish were kept.

The new king and queen moved from Kensington Palace into the Palace of Whitehall and Lady Powis waited on the queen in her new suite of rooms. Mary Beatrice was not altogether happy there. The grim knowledge of her father-in-law's beheading could not be eradicated by the redecoration: he had walked to his death from the drawing room and it was said that the stain of his blood could not be wiped from the floor. Impressive though her rooms were, with ceilings newly painted by Italian artists, magnificent marble fireplaces and gilded carving, she still hankered after the dark, creaking rooms of St James's Palace where, in spite of the draughts, she and her ladies had enjoyed themselves sitting over sea-coal fires, playing at cards. She took little pleasure from life at court, with its masques, balls and entertainments which she was now obliged to attend.

Perhaps as a result of their boyhood in exile, both Charles and James indulged themselves to excess. Passionate about women and sport they hunted voraciously and gaming, drinking and whoring became royal pastimes. Under Charles, the open, rollicking court at the Palace of Whitehall had sunk to a low level and James had been asked by his chaplain to raise the moral standard there. To this end he ordered his brother's mistress, the Duchess of Portsmouth, to remove herself from the palace and return to her native France. His own mistress, the ugly but witty Catherine Sedley, now the mother of his only surviving son, was banished to St James's Square, only a short walk away. However, when the child became ill and eventually died, James went to comfort her and soon she was back in court just as before.

James was as passionate about his religion as he was about the pleasures of the flesh and lost no time in adding a Catholic chapel to Whitehall. It was splendidly decorated by Grinling Gibbons with festoons of carvings and statues of white marble, and the extravagant ceremony at the high masses celebrated there astounded the diarist, John Evelyn. He listened in amazement to a full Italian choir singing in Latin, and watched incredulously through the incense-filled air as three Jesuits "censed the bishop" and made "diverse cringes" on the altar. He came away "not believing I should ever have lived to see such things in the King of England's Palace".

It was of course the absence of any legitimate living heirs that allowed the country to tolerate their Catholic king and queen at all. Mary Beatrice had been married twelve years and given birth seven times but her offspring had either died as babies or in their childhood, and it was generally held that she was incapable of having a healthy child. This would leave the Protestant Mary or, failing her, Anne, James's daughters by his first wife, Anne Hyde, to eventually inherit the Crown.

Although the country may have come to this conclusion, the royal pair themselves had not given up all hope of producing an heir. To aid her fertility Mary Beatrice paid several visits to Bath. There she bathed in the waters, watched over by Lady Powis and the ladies of the court while an Italian string quartet played in the background.

Her faith was rewarded. In the summer of 1687, to the surprise of everyone, she became pregnant. Catholics all over Britain were overjoyed and at once offered up prayers for the safe delivery of a healthy child while scurrilous broadsheets proclaimed that either the pregnancy was a lie or, if not, that the king was not really the father. The commanding Lady Powis watched over the queen like a mother hen, determined that this baby would be born and would live. She fended off visitors who pestered her and tried to keep ugly rumours from her ears.

The pregnancy came as an unpleasant shock to Princess Anne and her sister Mary, now married to Prince William of Orange. Should the baby be a boy they would no longer be the next heirs to the Crown and Britain would be subjected to a Catholic king. Anne gleefully reported any scandalous rumours to her sister in Holland and became cool towards the stepmother who had shown her nothing but kindness.

As the time of the birth approached, Mary Beatrice appeared to be more and more depressed. Haunted by thoughts of the babies and children who had not lived, she became pessimistic about the survival of this one and began to yearn for her old home of St James's. Finally, it was suggested that she return there for the birth and so, a few days before the baby was due, the state bedroom was hastily opened up, the great bed was aired with a large warming-pan, and, on a warm June evening, she was carried through the park on a litter, lest the movement of a coach should bring on her labour.

Lord and Lady Powis were amongst the mass of spectators who had been assembled to witness the birth and the king sat by the bedside. To hide her embarrassment from the gaze of so many eyes, the poor queen hid her face in her husband's periwig. Finally, after a long and painful labour, the midwife, smiling with delight, made a prearranged sign to the king which signified that it was a boy, and a gentleman of the Bedchamber took the tiny baby from her and, holding him high above his head, carried him into an ante-chamber crying triumphantly "make way for the Prince of Wales".

In spite of the many witnesses, the news of the prince's birth was received with even more scepticism than the pregnancy. Now it was said that the baby had been smuggled into the bed inside the warming-pan. Why, after all, should a bed need to be warmed on a hot June day? When the queen, terrified that the newborn baby would catch an infection, refused to show him off to visitors, suspicion only increased.

Lady Powis was appointed royal governess and entrusted with the child's welfare but it was not long before she realised that something was wrong: the baby was losing weight and refusing to feed. The doctors believed that it was milk which had caused the queen's other babies, convulsions and recommended a diet of canary wine and water gruel, but still the little prince cried all day and vomited continually. The doctors conferred and decided to add barley, oatmeal, sugar and currants to his gruel but his condition deteriorated rapidly and the king and queen were beginning to resign themselves to the fact that they could not produce a healthy child. As a last resort they ordered Lady Powis to take him in the royal coach to Richmond to see if he would benefit from country air. When they bade the little prince goodbye, his parents believed it might be the last time they would see him alive.

However, once away from the doctors, Lady Powis took matters into her own hands, sending orders for a wet nurse to be waiting for them. A young woman was found and as soon as she arrived the child was put to her breast. "It is incredible the amount of matter vomited from that tiny body at the first taste of milk", wrote an onlooker, but from that moment James Edward's health improved. His sudden recovery spawned yet more rumours, and it was suggested that he was either the wet nurse's baby or that he was the child of Mary Grey, one of the queens's gentlewomen.

A healthy Catholic prince was not what the country wanted. James held himself remote from his people and without considering public feeling he ordered a Declaration of Indulgence, allowing freedom of worship for all religions, to be read from the pulpit of every church. When seven bishops refused to obey these orders they were thrown into prison. The king had gone too far and negotiations were started with William and Mary in Holland. The Protestant William of Orange, ambitious to further his aims in Europe, lost no time in preparing his fleet to set sail for England.

CHAPTER 3

Exile

But let us talk of the King and Queen of England. It is such an extraordinary thing to have this court here that nothing else is spoken of.
MADAME DE SÉVIGNÉ.

On a freezing cold December night a small group of poorly-dressed men and women stood huddled together by the riverside at Gravesend. They carried with them what appeared to be all their belongings, packed in shabby bundles. Amongst them was a washerwoman, the shawl that covered her head pulled well down over her face, and her arms tightly clasping a load of dirty washing. One by one they silently boarded a waiting boat which made its way down the dark Thames and proceeded to cross the Channel to France.

Although the captain may not have known when he set sail who his passengers were, by the time he reached France he realised that he had on board none other than the Queen of England herself, carrying the baby prince in her arms, accompanied by Lord and Lady Powis and the rest of her ladies and gentlemen. As the boat pitched and rolled through the icy waters, skilfully avoiding the Dutch fleet, Lord and Lady Powis knew that they were leaving behind them their children, their country and all their possessions but faithful service to their king and queen was more important to them than personal attachments.

Soon after the royal party arrived on the other side of the Channel they were joined by James himself. France was familiar territory to both James and Mary Beatrice. James had stayed for a while with his mother, Queen Henrietta Maria, when she had returned to her native country during the Civil War. He had fought with the French army and had achieved a reputation for bravery.

Mary Beatrice had been received by Louis in more recent and happier times, when she had passed through France from Italy on her way to marry James. Now the exiles were welcomed by the great Sun King with every ceremony. He was delighted to have the English king on his soil as a declared ally since William of Orange was the block to Louis' ambitions on the Continent and he hoped that together they could chase William out of England and crush his strength in Europe once and for all.

The imposing palace of St Germain-en-Laye, which Louis placed at James's disposal, stood on a plateau, high above a bend in the River Seine. From the outside it was a vast,

Chateau Vieux, St Germain-en-Laye, north west façade. Photograph: Man de St Germain-en-Laye, C. Hamon.

forbidding building with endless lines of tall, narrow windows. Inside, over-shadowed by the high walls, was a gloomy courtyard. Louis had spent much of his childhood there and had only recently forsaken the chateau for his new creation at Versailles. While he had lived at St Germain he had improved it as much as possible, creating parterre gardens with intricately patterned flower beds which lay to the east, towards the Bois de Boulogne, and instructing Le Nôtre, the famous landscape gardener, to make a terrace stretching for a mile and a half, overlooking the Seine. From here, on a clear day, the spires of Paris could be seen in the distance. Cut into the rocky bank of the river were elaborate grottos. In the days of Mary of Medici, engineers had been brought from Italy to fill them with life-size mechanical figures who could walk and bow at their admiring audience.

Louis made every effort to make the Palace as comfortable as possible for its new occupants. His own apartments had been made ready for the English king and queen and another suite of rooms had been decorated as nurseries for the baby prince, to be under the charge of Lady Powis, the official royal governess. Nothing had been overlooked. The castle was staffed with servants and chefs of the highest order who could prepare mouth-watering dishes for the English exiles. When the queen was shown into her own room she found a casket containing 6000 gold coins lying on her dressing table. It was a useful gift but also a blunt reminder that they were now dependent on the hospitality of France.

James's court increased daily. England had divided into Jacobites and Williamites and many of the former, with hardly a penny between them, had decided to join their king. The French pension shrank in the face of such numbers and it was obvious that

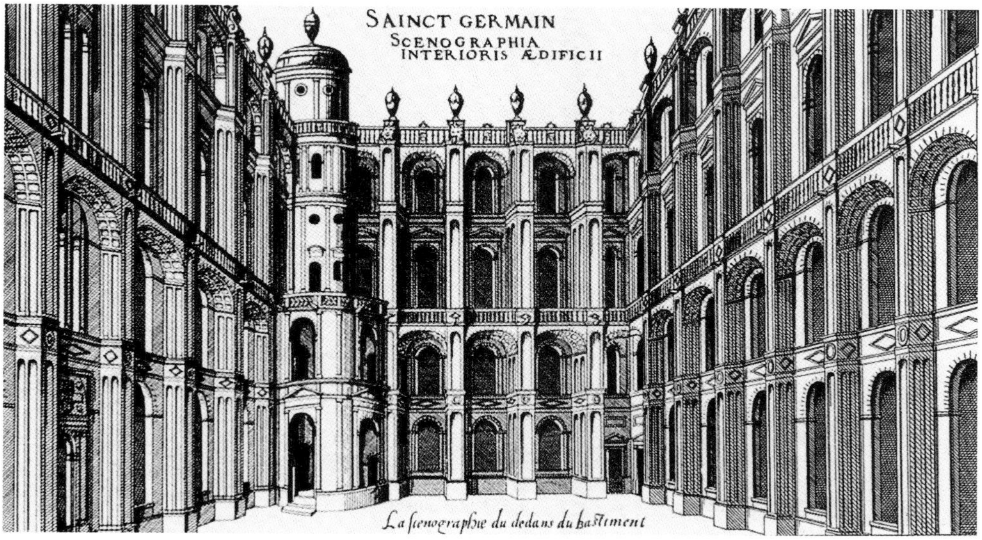

Chateau Vieux, St Germain-en-Laye inner courtyard. Photograph: MAN de St Germain-en-Laye, C. Hamon.

economies had to be made. The French chefs were replaced by English cooks who could provide plain food in vast quantities. The gentlemen soon became so bored with their diet that they hunted everything that moved and the locals began to complain that there was nothing left in the forest that could walk or fly.

These ill-clad, impoverished exiles were a source of great interest to the French court, and those who were invited to hunting parties at Marly, fêtes at Trianon or to balls held at the glittering palace of Versailles, were scrutinised mercilessly. Queen Mary Beatrice met with more approval than her husband, exciting admiration for her tall, slender figure, fine black eyes and beautiful teeth. It was also noted that Louis held her in great esteem and it was always prudent to share the monarch's taste. "This is how a queen ought to be" he told them, "both in person and mind holding her court with dignity." James, on the other hand, they found difficult to fathom. He was now in his late fifties and seemed older. Tall and fair-complexioned with a long, thin face he appeared to have shrunk in stature since his flight into exile and his stutter, which had become more pronounced, discouraged him from making conversation. The French formed the impression that he was not as intelligent as his wife and some even observed that they were not surprised that he was in his present situation.

The worldly courtiers of Louis XIV were amazed that the Jacobites could accept their fate and talk about their misfortunes so lightly. How could they still eat and drink and appear to be merry when, overnight, all their material goods had been left on the other side of the Channel? Lord Powis had even been heard discussing the loss of his wealth and vast estates while consuming large quantities of turkey and ham.

The exiles, of course, were still keeping up their spirits by believing that their stay in France was only temporary. Later in life Mary Beatrice confessed that she had tried at first to imagine that she was on a pleasurable holiday and that if, at that time, she had known otherwise, she did not know how she would have borne it.

Meanwhile, William and Mary appeared in London "riant and jolly as if to a wedding" and ensconced themselves in the Palace of Whitehall, which they had no intention of vacating. Mary was said to be perfectly at home among her step-mother's possessions and had even tried to fit her plump figure into her clothes. They were quite prepared to be amiable to their predecessors and when William heard that James and Mary Beatrice missed their own coach and horses he offered to have them sent over. Mary Beatrice's arrived first, complete with her coachman, but before her huband's could be dispatched William had heard that James intended to fight him in Ireland and he reconsidered the offer.

The Jacobites were convinced that their most likely way back to Britain would be by way of Ireland, where there were supposed to be a large number of supporters ready to fight for their cause. Louis, anxious to help, supplied frigates, arms and money to finance the expedition which was to end in the famous Battle of the Boyne. Lord Powis accompanied James as Louis sent them on their way with the following words: "You cannot say that I am not affected at your departure, I own to you however that I wish never to see you again. But if unfortunately you should return be assured you will find me as you leave me."

Hopes were high as the English set sail for Ireland in the boats that the French had provided. Lord Powis was among the king's party which landed at Kinsale and made its way to Dublin, where they were welcomed with bonfires and ringing bells, and where the king made an impressive entry into the castle with four bishops holding a canopy over his head. Here Lord Powis received Louis' ambassador extraordinary, d'Avaux, and James officially expressed his gratitude for the French assistance.

The Irish gave the army lavish hospitality and the Jacobites reciprocated with balls and dinners. However, when James and his army finally came up against William's troops at Oldbridge, near the mouth of the River Boyne, they were no match for the British. The Jacobites suffered a devastating defeat and returned to France humiliated, while French soldiers brought back scathing accounts of James's conduct on the battlefield and tarnished his earlier reputation for bravery.

It was at this point that the Jacobite exiles realised that their sojourn in France might be longer than they had anticipated. Lord Powis was made Lord High Chamberlain and had to deal with the exiles who were coming over in a steady stream; English, Scots and now, after the Battle of the Boyne, Irish too.

A sad economy took place when the 150 defeated Scottish officers who had attempted a rising on behalf of James in Scotland at Killiecrankie, and who had formed his military household at St Germain, realised that they could no longer be supported. They asked the king's permission to leave him and join the French army as ordinary soldiers. A poignant ceremony was carried out in the courtyard of the castle, as James reviewed his bodyguard for the last time. He walked down the rows thanking each man personally and writing down his name in a notebook. The whole company then knelt down, bowed low and gave a final royal salute.

Though the arrival of the English was still "a constant subject for conversation", as Madame de Sévigné wrote to her daughter, and it was fascinating for the French to have in their midst a man who was prepared to "lose three crowns for a mass", it had also become necessary to work out the order of precedence when the court at Versailles mixed with their own. King Louis had kept secret his marriage to his middle-aged mistress, Madame de Maintenon, and so, though unofficially she reigned supreme, she could not be included in the official rank. His son's wife, the Dauphine, was the first lady and was none too pleased to be told that on social occasions the Queen of England must now take precedence over her. To emphasise her position, she refused to admit Lord Powis to her rooms one morning when he had been sent by Mary Beatrice to enquire after her health. She told Louis firmly that she was unable to receive anyone as lowly as a marquess. When James granted Lord Powis a dukedom, she was unable to quibble further.

The new duke's position as Lord Chamberlain was not becoming any easier. The palace was bursting at the seams with discordant and discontented exiles. There were quarrels between the English and the Scots and between the Catholics and the Protestants, who had all supported James for different reasons. The Protestant "Non Jurors" were Jacobites because they believed in the unbroken succession of kings, while the Catholics wished for civil rights and freedom to practise their religion. Each person had in addition more complex reasons of their own for choosing exile. Their insecurity and poverty exacerbated their differences and led to continual jealousies and squabbles.

The announcement that Queen Mary Beatrice was expecting another child brought a welcome diversion, and the new Duchess of Powis found herself with an added responsibility. Besides the welfare of the little prince, the apple of his parents' eye, she also had to watch over the health of Mary Beatrice. The Powis's had already sent for their daughter Lucy, who had been taken into the queen's service, and they now sent for their youngest daughter Winifred.

JAMES II's DESCENDANTS

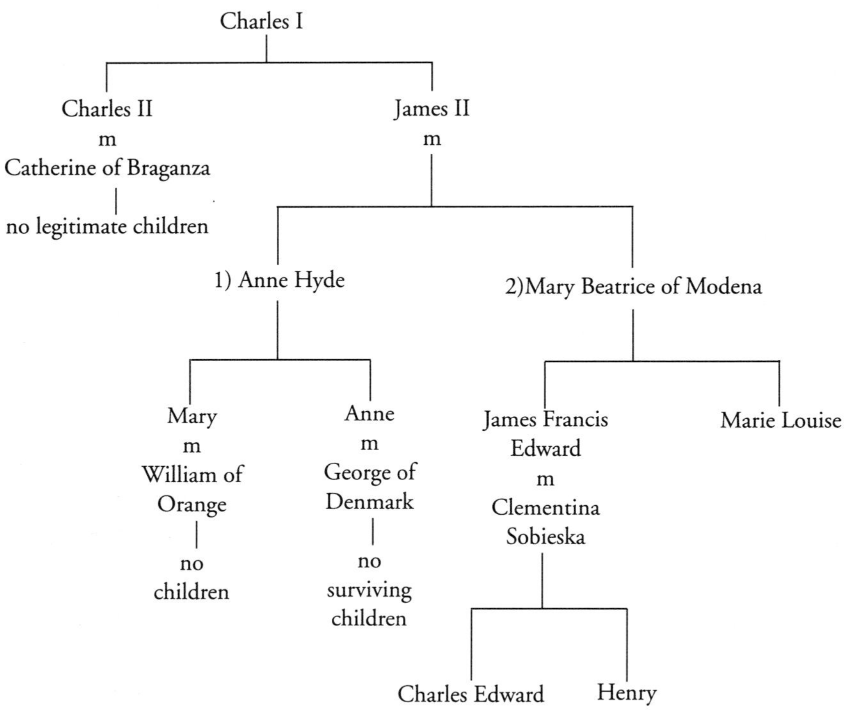

CHAPTER 4

St Germain-en-Laye

In the late autumn of 1691, a pass was obtained for "Lady Winifred Herbert and two servants" to travel to France. Since her parents had left England three years before, it is most likely that Winifred had been put into the care of her married sisters, Mary, now Lady Molyneux, or Anne who was deeply involved in Jacobite intrigue, and who had married a rich widower many years older than herself, Francis Smith, Viscount Carrington. Her other sister, Frances Seaforth had also suffered for the cause. Her Scots husband had been incarcerated in Edinburgh Castle and she had obtained permission to join him there. Their brother, William, had been apprehended and put into the Tower of London: as the son of a prominent Jacobite, he was too dangerous a young man be left on the loose. The mob had once again thrown stones through the windows of their house in Lincoln's Inn Fields, and their great castle in Wales had been taken into the possession of the new king.

The nineteen-year-old Winifred who arrived at the "dreadfullest place in Europe next to the Bastille" was a slender, pretty girl with fair skin and wide-apart brown eyes which disguised the steely determination shared by all the Herbert sisters. She was accompanied by Cecilia Evans, the daughter of an army officer from Welshpool. This stalwart young woman was to be her companion through all the vicissitudes of her life.

The joy of being reunited with her parents and her favourite sister Lucy was marred by Lucy's announcement that she that she had made up her mind to become a nun, and, sadder still, would go to a convent many miles away in Flanders. Lucy disliked life at court and had no desire to marry. She had resisted pressure, both from the queen and her parents to join the less strict Visitation convent at nearby Chaillot and had decided instead, under the influence of the queen's chaplain, Father de Sabran, to enter a contemplative order, the English Augustine nuns at Bruges. She intended to go there as soon as the queen's baby was born.

Winifred found her mother in poor health. Lady Powis was middle-aged and worn down by her duties, but still determined to take full responsibility for the prince and the forthcoming child. The four-year-old Prince James Edward, who, it was said, had been cured of rickets by being tossed in the air regularly, was a fine healthy child and preparations for the new baby were under way.

The prospect of a new prince or princess, as well as the rumour of a fresh opportunity to attempt a restoration, had lifted the exiles' spirits. It was known that James had

Prince James Francis Edward by Nicholas de Largilliere (Scottish National Portrait Gallery)

secretly left St Germain and news was being passed around that another attack was to be made, this time on the Dutch. James was to command French ships and take on the combined Dutch and British navy at sea. His skill when he had been Lord High Admiral with the British fleet was still remembered and hopes were high for success.

However, the possiblity of a restoration also brought new disputes about how James ought to act, should he be victorious and return to England. There were some who were in favour of granting a general amnesty and the retention of civil liberties, while others were against any sort of compromise. James finally came down on the side of the moderates and a general amnesty was drafted to be proclaimed in England should it be needed.

This was not to be. The battle which took place at Cap de La Hogue, painful for James in any case, as he found himself in combat with the British Fleet which he had previously commanded, was another dismal failure. The French ships soon found themselves to be well outnumbered. It did not take long for the French fleet under his command to be overcome and, as an added humiliation, the Dutch penetrated right into the harbour where the ships lay and destroyed some of them.

Before James returned home, Queen Mary Beatrice gave birth and on his arrival, a healthy baby girl was put into the arms of the elderly father. Weary and dejected, he clasped his daughter to him saying to his wife, "God has given her to us to be our consolation". He was later heard to say that at last he had a daughter who had shown him no unkindness.

In sharp contrast to James's defeat, Louis returned victorious from a land battle against the Dutch at Namur. As was the custom when victory was expected, over fifty French ladies of the court, complete with their children, maids and diamonds, had set out on foot for the battlefield to witness their king's glory and they came back singing his praises.

The birth of the Stuart princess was received with great jubilation by the Jacobites. Not only did it give them a second heir should James be restored to the throne, but they felt it refuted once and for all the myth that the queen was not capable of bearing healthy children and thus conclusively proved the legitimacy of the prince.

The christening took place in the Chapel Royal at St Germain in great splendour, and an invitation was triumphantly extended to (but not accepted by) the childless William and Mary and their Privy Council across the Channel. The Duchess of Orleans, the wife of Monsieur, Louis' younger brother, was Godmother and, as Louis himself agreed to stand godfather, the baby princess was christened Louise Marie in his honour. The French ladies twittered in amazement to see the month-old princess clothed like a miniature adult in a robe of satin and lace and wearing minute shoes and stockings, quite unlike a French baby, who would have been tightly swaddled and bound to a cushion.

Having remained with the queen until after her baby was born, Lucy kept to her word and the following winter, accompanied by Father de Sabran, took leave of her family and set off through the snows on her journey to the convent in Bruges. The fact that France and Holland were still at war and there could be no communication between Lucy and her family, made the parting even sadder. Winifred's distress increased when, a few months later, her mother became ill and died.

The queen, who had lost one of her longest-serving ladies, immediately took her forlorn daughter Winifred into her service. Accommodation was allotted according to rank and it seems likely that, as an unmarried lady, she was given Lucy's small turret room leading off one of the tight spiral stairs that ran up each corner of the building. She would have received her orders during daily visits to the Queen's apartments which were situated on the first floor of the palace. Under Louis' instruction they were were enhanced all the year by great bouquets of fresh flowers, in the finest porcelain vases, delivered daily from his greenhouses at Versailles. The rooms were connected to James's dark-green and gold apartments and to the royal nurseries by a wide balcony on which Louis had stood to watch his hounds, but which now served as a private playground for the young prince.

The king and queen had become devoted to each other during their years in exile and the king was now as deeply religious as his wife. The queen liked nothing better than to spend a few days with the nuns at the convent at Chaillot, where she put on a habit and was treated as their reverend mother. The king, making up for his ill-spent youth, stayed with the monks at the monastery of La Trappe where he shared their mortifications, learnt to sit in a room without a fire and to wear a hair shirt next to his skin. To the regret of his courtiers, he expected them to follow his new exemplary way of life and began to discourage theatrical entertainments or the reading of light books. Invitations to entertainments at Versailles and Marly were accepted less readily, much to the disappointment of the bored exiles who craved diversion. It was noted with relief that both the king and queen each reserved one pleasure. The queen still enjoyed her games of cards and the king still indulged in his favourite drink, champagne.

In the autumn of 1696 Lord Powis fell from his horse while riding back from Paris through the Bois de Boulogne. He was carried into the palace where he lay sick and despondent. A visit to the king's favourite waters was suggested but he returned no better and his decline increased until he was not expected to live. During this final illness he was obsessed by the thought that he had not treated his youngest daughter well, and that he would leave her with no means of support and no husband. Winifred was now twenty-five and by that age her three sisters had all been married to eligible husbands. Their circumstances had of course been very different, since they had been the daughters of an influential nobleman who could provide them with a substantial dowry.

Chateau Vieux, St Germain-en-Laye, showing royal apartments on first floor.
Photograph: MAN de St Germain-en-Laye, C. Hamon.

In his sickness he began to suffer from scruples and felt that he had been "harsh and unkind" in his treatment of her and he poured out his worries to the priest who tended him in his last days. A previous will had left what little he had to his son, William, but now he was determined to make amends to Winifred. When the priest told Winifred of her father's intention she tried to dissuade him, being well aware of the discord this might cause between herself and her brother. However, the day before his death he insisted on altering his will in her favour and leaving Winifred the last remaining piece of his wife's jewellery.

After her father's death, the queen began to regard Winifred as a daughter, or younger sister since there was only 10 years difference in their ages. She accompanied the queen to Versailles and Marly and learned the strict etiquette of the French court, where even seating arrangements were of the utmost importance. Armchairs (fauteuils) were reserved for the highest rank only, armless chairs were for lesser royalty and upholstered stools were for anyone else who was actually allowed to be seated. She witnessed the arrival of the doll-like Marie Adelaide of Savoy who came as a child bride to marry the young Duc de Bourgogne, Louis' eldest grandson. This pretty creature fascinated the court to such an extent that it became the fashion for everyone to play childish games.

James and Mary Beatrice had made a long list of rules for their own prince's upbringing: he was not allowed to receive gifts of food, flowers, perfume or sweet water without his governor's leave; whispering to the prince and private conversation with him were forbidden; any writing or books, and all songs, must pass the governor's censorship; no uninvited children must visit him, and not more than three or four companions should play with him at the same time.

These rules were made for good reason. Among the court were exiles who were prepared to use the child to gain information or put forward a plea and James had many visitors from England who came to find out how the land lay and were terrified lest it be known they had made contact with the Jacobites. When the prince was only four years old, Lord Aylesbury had come over in great secrecy from England to visit James. The whole court had been dying to know the identity of the influential gentleman who had been carried through the palace in a sedan chair with the curtains firmly closed. They questioned the prince who had seen the stranger talking to his father, and the little boy's description of him as "very large" had enabled the courtiers to guess correctly who it had been.

As the years passed James Edward grew up to be a handsome, serious-minded boy admired for his self-possessed manner and skills both at his books and out hunting. In the opinion of his governor, the Duke of Perth, he was "full of every charm that can engage hearts". His sister, Louise Marie, was in contrast a carefree, fun-loving child, adored by the whole court. When taken to the opera at the age of four she accompanied the singers in lusty tones, to the admiration of all. But Mary Beatrice never let her children forget the plight of the exiles around them. She set an example by asking her ladies to only give her the same dishes to eat as the rest of the court and once chided

Lady Strickland, the under governess who took Lady Powis' place, for presenting her with a specially prepared dish of partridges. Both her children were encouraged from an early age to save up their pocket-money for the needy.

James had lost both his ambition and his vigour, and his return to the English throne seemed ever less likely, as Louis was forced to conclude. Louis' own campaign against the Dutch was faring badly and, to the Jacobites' chagrin, in 1697 he signed the Treaty of Ryswick with William and agreed to acknowledge him as King of Great Britain. In compensation, William at last agreed to pay Mary Beatrice's jointure of £50,000 which had been settled on her by an Act of Parliament twelve years before but which she had never received. This in fact did not materialise.

William's wife, Mary, had died a few years previously and he was now a childless widower. The heir to the English Crown was therefore his sister-in-law, Anne. Of the seventeen children she had borne, only one survived, the delicate little Duke of Gloucester. William had never doubted James's legitimacy and maintained that when he looked at his portrait he could see his uncle Charles's mouth and his mother's eyes. In an attempt to settle the succession he made the suggestion that the young prince should be sent to England and brought up as a Protestant so that he could inherit the throne. But both James and Mary Beatrice refused to consider this proposition.

CHAPTER 5

Scotland

In the spring of 1699, a young Scots nobleman arrived at the Palace of St Germain-en-Laye to pay his respects to his Stuart king. William Maxwell was both the 5th Earl of Nithsdale and the 8th Baron Herries. He came from an ancient Royalist and Jacobite family and had succeeded to the title as a child. At the age of sixteen he had received an order from the exiled James to take up arms on his behalf, and also a royal appointment as colonel of a cavalry regiment. But as, at that time, the Jacobites had not succeeded in instigating a rebellion in the south of Scotland, his military duties had so far not been called upon. This was no disappointment to him for he did not have a natural inclination to take up the sword.

Lord Nithsdale by John Medina.

He was a well-built, fashionably-dressed young gentleman with large brown eyes and ruddy cheeks and a wig of dark, curling hair. He wore cravats of fine muslin and the sought-after English stockings; it was obvious that he took great pleasure in his clothes. His manners also were impeccable and he danced elegantly, for his widowed mother had taken care that he should be suitably accomplished. Extra masters had been called in to teach him French and history as well as fencing and dancing. There may well have been an added incentive for his journey to St Germain. One of his mother's sisters had been the Duke of Perth's first wife and the two families had remained firm friends. Since her father's death, the duke and duchess had taken Winifred under their wing and the sage couple would not have missed the opportunity of bringing two young people from the same background and religion together. The fact that Winifred had a small dowry would also not have passed unnoticed.

After he had been introduced to Winifred, William wasted little time before asking for her hand in marriage. They were attracted to each other and both knew that it was a suitable match. Among the many things they had in common was the fact that both their families had remained faithful to the Stuart kings and the Catholic religion and had suffered for that loyalty.

Winifred at twenty-seven, was four years older than William, but suitors at the court of St Germain were few and she had no inclination to follow her sister into a convent. The offer from this personable young Scotsman was too good to refuse and after she had made a short retreat in the Benedictine convent at Pontoise they were married quietly in Paris.

The young groom was in no hurry to take his bride home to Scotland. Always partial to the good things of life, he found Paris in the company of his beautiful wife much to his taste. He was treated with respect at the court of St Germain, where his importance as one of the most influential Jacobites in the south west of Scotland was recognised, and for a young man who had previously only received deprivations in return for his loyalty to the Stuart crown, it was gratifying to have his fealty appreciated.

It is unlikely that William's true financial position was known to Winifred at the start of their married life. He dressed extravagantly, dined well and appeared to have enough money for them both to live comfortably. She knew he had an estate at home and he drew bills on it at will. After their marriage, as was the custom, a jointure was drawn up whereby all her money became his but, should she outlive him, a proportion of the money would be returned to her.

In fact, William was at this time beginning to receive letters from his factor, a cousin, Maxwell of Munches, urging him to return home as soon as possible to deal with his far from satisfactory financial affairs. Reluctantly, he was prevailed upon to do so and to prepare for their journey back to Scotland. Winifred said her farewells to the king and queen and their children and, accompanied by her constant companion the devoted Evans, left the palace which had been her home for the last nine years. They crossed the Channel to England and made their way to London and to the lodgings "at the white balcony in Duke Street" owned by a Mrs Mills, who had become a family friend.

Here Winifred, who was now in the early stages of pregnancy, fell ill. She always inspired great affection in those who served her and was nursed with every care by Evans and Mrs Mills. As Winifred lay ill in bed, William received another letter from Munches who told him that a bill was waiting to be paid by the 24th of the month "but where the money shall be had to do it I do not know for I know of none to borrow and from the bank it cannot be expected". He hoped that his lordship would "hasten home for if you come not immediately and settle with your creditors they will both ruin your Lordships credit and put you to much needless trouble and a great deal of expense". On the same day Munches confided to a friend that he was receiving so much torment from Lord Nithsdale's creditors that he was sure "the meanest ploughman in the land has had a more contented life than I since he went away".

Before they left town a sad piece of news was announced. Princess Anne's only surviving son, the Duke of Gloucester, had died. His eleventh birthday had been celebrated with a ball at Kensington Palace and it was thought that he had caught a chill after becoming over-heated and then smallpox had set in. The whole country went into mourning and the courts at Versailles and St Germain decided to do likewise. James had ignored the death of his daughter Mary, much to the contempt of the French who found his attitude small-minded, but her treatment of him had left a lasting scar. He allowed, however, that his grandson's case was quite different as "the tender age of the prince prevented him from having any share in the crime of rebellion and usurpation against his grandfather".

The death of the duke left Prince James Edward heir to his two half-sisters as well as to his father, with a three-fold claim to the throne of England. There was a surge of confidence among Jacobites all over the country. They openly sported white cockades in the streets and publicly raised their glasses to the king over the water. Lord Manchester wrote in alarm to the Secretary of State that "seven thousand medals of the Pretender Prince of Wales are to be stamped by Rotier".

Meanwhile, under the loving care of Mrs Mills and Cecilia Evans, Winifred gradually recovered her health and William, buoyed up by the political news, decided that they should make the journey north. His castle, Terregles, stood among the hills in the south west of Scotland and, if a hard winter set in, the road to it would soon beecome impassable.

Silver Medal by Norbert Roettier showing Prince James Edward Stuart (Drambuie Collection).

Scotland, at the start of the eighteenth century, was in poor shape. Unlike England, the country was verging on bankruptcy. Several years of bad weather had followed hard upon each other, with extreme winters and cold, sunless summers. Crops had not ripened and had been left to rot in the fields, unharvested. Poverty could be seen everywhere; on the faces of the poor and hungry, the beggars who tramped the roads, the deserted houses in the villages and the emaciated corpses of animals who lay unburied, dead from starvation. Added to that, the Darien scheme, a Scottish colonial project for which great hopes had been raised, had failed, and a large amount of investment had been lost, affecting the very roots of the economy.

English travellers of the time were aware that they were in a different country as soon as they crossed the border. They saw no beauty in the unenclosed land. "The huge naked rocks being just above the heath produce the disagreeable appearance of a scabbed head" complained Celia Fiennes, a contemporary writer, "and the whole of a dismal brown drawing upon a dirty purple and most of all disagreeable when the heath is in bloom." This intrepid traveller balked at staying in Scotland, where she had heard that "even nobleman's houses, though all kind of castles, are lived in so nasty a kind of way that one has little stomach to eat or use anything".

Not only did Winifred have to acclimatise herself to a different way of life, but she was also going to live in a country where her religious beliefs were not tolerated and those who still practised Catholicism were treated with severity. Religious differences had torn Scotland apart. Until 1690 Episcopalianism had been the established church and under James II the Covenanters, a Presbyterian splinter group based mainly in the south west, had been viciously suppressed by the king's troops led by Claverhouse, or "Bonnie Dundee". William's father, the 4th Earl of Nithsdale, had been rebuked for not taking sterner measures against them in Nithsdale, though he had benefited from some of the Covenanters' sequestered land. After the arrival of William and Mary, Presbyterianism had become the established church and a backlash was taking place. The Covenanters, who had now mostly rejoined the Presbyterians, had driven the Episcopalian ministers from their manses and were also persecuting the Catholics, and the penal laws were being enforced with renewed vigour. In spite of this, a Jesuit priest, Father Innes, was kept in secret at Terregles as chaplain for the family and as a priest, to minister to all the Catholics in the area.

The castle of Terregles was very different from the noble castle of Powis where Winifred had spent her childhood. It was a high Scots tower house with thick walls, low ceilings and a few small windows. The building had been extended when defence was no longer so necessary and the new rooms, some of them panelled, were larger and looked into an oval-shaped courtyard. The old tower had in fact narrowly escaped being razed to the ground 150 years earlier when the Regent Moray marched triumphantly through the countryside destroying the castle of anyone he suspected of opposing him. The Lord

The old tower house of Terregles.

Herries of the day was known to be a loyal supporter of Mary, Queen of Scots and a certain target for the Regent's wrath. His castle was saved only by the wit of his uncle, the laird of Drumlanrig, who told the Regent that his nephew was intending to pull down his house anyway in order to rebuild. The Regent immediately swore that he refused to "be a barrowman to his old walls" and had let it stand.

The new bride found the household in the capable hands of her mother-in-law, Lucie Douglas, who had managed the affairs of the family and estate since her husband's death seventeen years previously. She had been successful in obtaining a pension from Charles II of £22 sterling for the "better maintenance of herself and her son and daughter" because of the "low condition of the family" and the "great burdens that lay on the estate". It was acknowledged that these were chiefly due to their loyalty during the "late troubles".

In former times their estates had been vast and the Maxwells had controlled the south of Scotland from their Castle of Caerlaverock like small kings. This fine building had been reduced to a ruin under Cromwell and the land that was left to them, at Terregles, brought in less than £1000 a year, mainly from rents and sales of barley, oatmeal, chickens and hens and a small amount of peat. Thrifty management and careful living might have freed the estate from its encumbrances, but it was not long before Winifred realised that this was not the manner in which her husband was able to live.

CHAPTER 6

The Union

Farewell thou ancient kingdom
Who sold thyself
For English pelf
Was ever such a thing done.

Soon after her arrival at Terregles, Winifred met William's sister Mary who was married to Charles Stuart, the 4th Earl of Traquair. His castle, Traquair, was in the Border country. It had originally been built on a bank above the river Tweed and was surrounded by the great oak trees of the Ettrick Forest. The river had since been diverted to run further from the building and the bank had been landscaped to form a double terrace.

TRAQUAIR CASTLE, PEEBLESSHIRE.

Mary Maxwell, 4th Countess of Traquair, Sir John Medina.

The two women were exactly the same age and soon became close friends. Mary had now been married for five years and was the mother of five young children (Lucy, Anne, Charles, William and John) and was pregnant with her sixth child. She was a pretty, gentle woman with fair skin and her brother's brown eyes. Warm and sympathetic, she was adored by her husband who was thirteen years her senior.

Charles, 4th Earl of Traquair, Sir John Medina.

Charles was not only dark and good-looking, but he was also man of integrity who was respected by his neighbours in spite of his known loyalty to the Catholic faith and the Stuart cause. He was astute enough to live quietly and had been able to preserve and improve his house and estate. His grandfather John, the 1st Earl of Traquair, had been an ally of Charles I and had tried to follow the king's wishes to bring his prayer book into Scotland. At the age of thirty-three he had been made Lord High Treasurer of

Scotland and had rapidly accumulated vast lands which had been lost as quickly with the collapse of the monarchy. Charles's father, the 2nd Earl had married the Catholic Lady Ann Seton who had converted the family back to the "true religion". Under Charles II they had, like the Maxwells, been rewarded for their loyalty to the Stuart cause and had been allowed "a little extra out of fines or forfeitures". This "extra" being meted out at the discretion of the Duke of Queensberry who was a kinsman and had taken a special interest in the family.

In the year 1700 both women gave birth to their babies. Mary's little girl died within a few months but Winifred's baby, a boy, another William, survived and was a great joy to both his parents and grandmother.

The following year news came through from France of the death of James II after a long period of ill health. Reports of the saintly manner of his death soon began to give rise to stories of cures that had been worked by his relics. It was a great relief to the Jacobites that, after James's death, the loyal Louis went back on the promises he had made to William in the Treaty of Ryswick, but kept the one he had made to James on his death-bed, and declared the young James Edward, now a boy of 13, "king of three kingdoms".

In England, King William was anxious to secure the succession of the monarchy to the Protestant line. As neither he nor his sister-in-law Anne had an heir, and his offer to James had been turned down, he ignored the fifty or more closer relations in line for the throne and wished the crown to pass to Sophia of Hanover, granddaughter of James VI and, after her, to her son George. He was worried that Scotland, as an independent country, did not need to have the same king as England and, for this reason above all was anxious to promote the idea of a union between the two countries. Before this could be accomplished "the little gentleman in black velvet", a mole, who was subsequently the toast at many a Jacobite dinner, ran in front of his mount bringing both horse and rider to the ground. Three weeks later King William was dead.

To the disappointment of the Jacobites, his sister-in-law, the Princess Anne, slipped onto the throne without apparent opposition. Although Scotland then passed the Act of Security which enabled the country at Anne's death to choose their own sovereign, the thought of Union with England was now firmly implanted in the minds of the Scottish leaders.

Meanwhile, Winifred's husband, William Nithsdale had returned from his visit to St Germain fired with renewed Jacobite sympathy. He had given his word that he was ready to take up arms when the time was ripe and was pledged to keep fidelity to the Jacobite cause alive to which end he carried on a busy correspondence under the pseudonym of Mr Nash. While he attended clandestine meetings and surreptitiously drank the health of King James at candlelit suppers, Winifred stayed at Terregles with her mother-in-law and her son William. Although she became pregnant again several times over the next few years the pregnancies resulted in miscarriages or babies that did not survive.

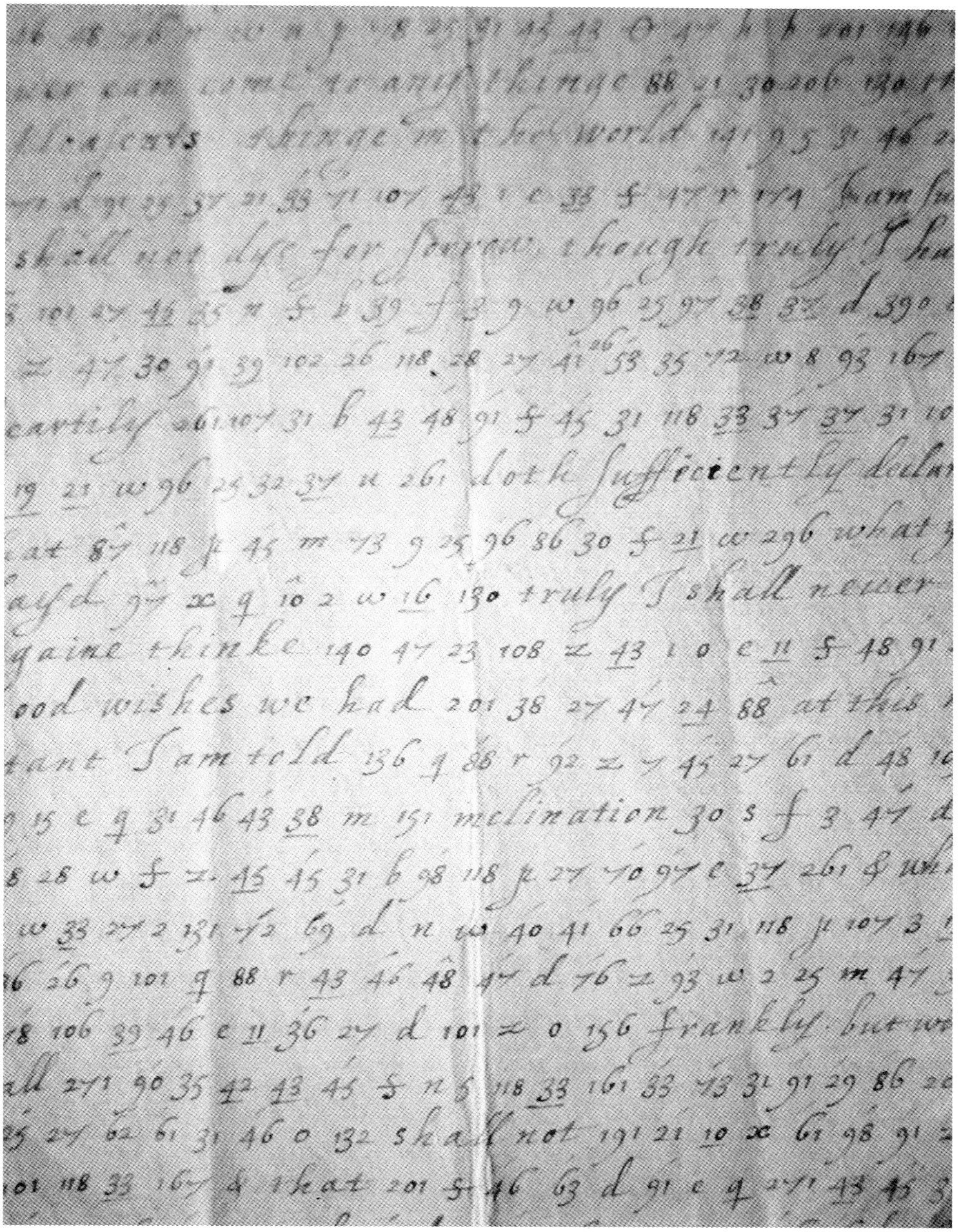
16 48 76 r w n f 78 25 31 43 43 O 47 h b 201 196
ever can come to any thinge 88 21 30 206 130
pleasants thinge in the world 141 95 31 46
and 91 25 37 21 38 71 107 43 1 e 33 f 47 r 174 I am su
shall not dye for sorrow, though truly I ha
5 101 27 43 35 n f b 39 f 3 9 w 96 25 97 38 37 d 390
z 47 30 91 39 102 26 118 28 27 41 53 35 72 w 8 93 167
eartily 261 107 31 b 43 48 91 f 45 31 118 33 37 37 31 10
19 21 w 96 25 32 37 n 261 doth sufficiently declar
at 87 118 p 45 m 73 9 25 96 86 30 f 21 w 296 what
ayd 97 x q 10 2 w 16 130 truly I shall never
gaine thinke 140 47 23 108 z 43 1 0 e 11 f 48 91
ood wishes we had 201 38 27 47 24 88 at this
tant I am told 136 q 88 r 92 z 7 45 27 61 d 48 10
9 15 e q 31 46 43 38 m 151 inclination 30 s f 3 47 d
8 28 w f z 45 45 31 b 98 118 p 27 70 97 e 37 261 & whi
w 33 27 2 131 72 69 d n w 40 41 66 25 31 118 p 107 3
76 26 9 101 q 88 r 43 46 48 47 d 76 z 93 w 2 25 m 47
78 106 39 46 e 11 36 27 d 101 z 0 156 frankly but w
all 271 90 35 42 43 45 f n 5 118 33 161 33 73 31 91 29 86
25 27 62 61 31 46 0 132 shall not 191 21 10 x 61 98 91
101 118 33 167 & that 201 f 46 63 d 91 e q 271 43 45

Jacobite letter in code.

It was on Christmas Eve 1703 that she experienced first-hand the terror of being a Catholic in a Covenanting part of the country. Feeling unwell that evening, she had retired to bed early. From her bedroom she began to hear the sounds of a rabble outside and looking out of the window saw a mob of at least a hundred people led by four local ministers. Armed with swords and guns they had first broken into the smithy where they had helped themselves to hammers and tools, and with these they had broken through both the outer and inner gates. Terrified and helpless the household heard them smash their way into the house, where they proceeded to search all the rooms. They found nothing, for the priest, knowing that Christmas was a dangerous time, had taken precautions and left, taking with him all his apparel. Finally, they hacked down the door of William's closet, hoping to get at his papers. Fortunately, he had taken the key of his chest with him to Edinburgh and again they were disappointed. They departed in frustration leaving the household in turmoil.

William was naturally furious when he heard what had happened and took proceedings against the ministers for their behaviour "so like and opposite to the spirit of the gospel". They were found guilty and fined 5000 merks Scots. The ministers, in their turn, then raised criminal letters against Lord Nithsdale for hearing mass and harbouring priests. They also alleged that, by the Act of Parliament of 1700 for the Prevention of the Growth of Popery, they had acted within the law. The proceedings took place in the Justiciary Court in Edinburgh and lasted for seven days. Lord Nithsdale was advised to come to a compromise with the ministers and, as a result, he was denuded of his office of heritable steward of Kirkcudbrightshire.

War had broken out between France and England, this time over the Spanish succession. Louis once again began to show an interest in supporting a Jacobite rebellion and restoring the young Stuart king to his throne. He was anxious to be certain that there were still enough nobles ready to rise if James landed and he instructed Colonel Nathanial Hooke, who was trusted both by the Jacobites at St Germain and the French court, to tour Scotland, interview the known sympathizers and see how many would commit themselves on paper.

Hooke travelled through the north of Scotland hoping to obtain signed promises of support from individual nobles. It proved to be a more difficult task than he had imagined, as James's supporters were not united. The majority were Episcopalian but there were also Cameronians and Catholics. Before the Union many professed themselves Jacobites merely because they were dissatisfied with the present state of affairs. A large number of Scottish nobles only wished to be on the winning side. It was difficult to pin them down, or in fact to meet them at all. This was an uncertain time and they were nervous that they might end up on the wrong side and were not at all anxious to sign their name to anything. Added to this, they were more than a little suspicious of French support, fearing that France's prime motive was to stir up trouble with England rather than a true desire to reinstate the Stuart king.

Several Scots declared themselves suddenly ill and unable to meet the Colonel. Lord Errol decided he had to leave home and left his wife, an ardent Jacobite, to receive Hooke in his place. She took the opportunity of offering her services as a spy and for many years kept up a correspondence with France, writing her letters in lemon juice. Another lady, the Duchess of Gordon, was equally willing to commit herself and devised a code which resembled a shopping list. "Scotch linen" meant England, "English broad cloth" meant Scotland, "French wines" was Presbyterians and "pepper" was ammunition.

Hooke returned to France filled with enthusiasm, but he had to admit that he would not be able to collect many signatures until the question of the Union of England and Scotland was settled. Relations between the two countries had gone from bad to worse. England had refused to allow Scotland to join in her overseas trade, and without this Scotland could not survive. When the English Parliament passed an Act of Settlement which declared that the Crown must pass to the nearest Protestant heir, Sophia, Electress of Hanover, the Scots played their last card and passed an Act of Security. This Act repudiated the Hanoverian succession unless Scotland was given full control of its Crown, Parliament, religion and trade. But England, knowing that the economic advantage was in their hands, responded to this with the Alien Act. The Scots were given less than a year to choose between being regarded as foreigners and debarred from trade with England or, agreeing to consider a union. Faced with this ultimatum, and fearing bankruptcy, Scotland was forced to enter into negotiations for a union.

The idea was unpopular with the majority of the people and the Jacobites, knowing that a union would prevent them from having a Stuart king, were violently opposed to it. Nevertheless, the wheels started to turn and Commissioners were appointed from each country to draw up the Treaty. The Scots went down to London and met their English counterparts in the cockpit, under the Palace of Westminster.

One of the Commissioners, John Clerk, a lawyer from the south of Scotland, noted "a great backwardness in the Parliament of Scotland for a union with England". He also noted that the Earl of Mar was "very forward for the Union and the settlement of succession in the Protestant family of Hanover". A noteworthy point, considering Mar's about turn later on. Clerk also visited the unfortunate Queen Anne in Kensington Palace where she was suffering from a severe fit of gout. She sat, "surrounded by plaisters cataplaims and dirty like rags, ill dressed and blotted in her countenance". He observed that she was pleased to receive anybody as no court attendants ever came near her. "All the incense and adoration offered at court were for her ministers."

In July 1706, the Articles of Union were signed and brought back to Edinburgh by the Commissioners. Clerk was surprised by the attitude of the people and commented, "the bulk of the nation seemed altogether averse to them". When the twelve wagons filled with English gold, the "bribe money", arrived in Edinburgh they were stoned by the mob, but, with true canniness, not until their load had first been deposited in the castle. It was thought that many of the nobles had received personal bribes to vote for the Union and, as soon as the Articles were signed, these gentlemen lost no time in making their way to London to see what well-paid positions they had gained for themselves.

CHAPTER 7

Attempt of 1708

As they had feared, Catholics received no comfort under the Union. The Presbyterian Church became the established church in Scotland, and limited toleration was granted only to those Episcopalians who were not Jacobite. Liberty of conscience and freedom to worship were refused to those of the Catholic faith. The change in the administration of justice made their lives even less secure. Circuit courts were now held regularly throughout the country and ministers were able to give information to the magistrates as to which families were harbouring priests and hearing mass. A reward was offered to informers and a number of priests and Catholic lay people were brought to trial.

Even in the Highlands where on the whole the Catholics were better treated, and where in some isolated areas they had still been able to run Catholic schools, the Privy Council had ordered that Lady Seaforth's son, should be taken away from her and sent to live with Presbyterian relations. She had managed instead to send him abroad to complete his education.

The Traquairs in the Borders were less troubled but the Nithsdales in Dumfriesshire were the object of continual scrutiny. Fearing for their own son's future, they were anxious to get William out of the country. Winifred's sister, Mary, had been twice widowed and had made a third marriage to a rich gentleman, Sir George Maxwell. He was in fact not related but as the couple had no children of their own, he had offered to be responsible for William's education. Plans were made to send him to school in France.

Disenchantment with the Union soon came from every side. A story was frequently told, after it had taken place, that a Scotsman travelling in England had asked an inn keeper's wife how safe the roads were. The good woman had smiled happily. There was no trouble now, she told him, as all the highwaymen had gone to Scotland to get a post. A large number of petty officials had indeed been taken on as tax collectors and customs officials, and had been sent up to Scotland where they threw their weight around and antagonised the Scots. The city of Edinburgh was also a different place. Previously, while a Scottish Parliament sat, it had been an important capital city where the nobility and Members of Parliament had taken town houses for the season, bringing their households with them. Balls and assemblies had been held and the streets and taverns had buzzed with gossip and thrived on a lively trade. Now the Houses of Parliament stood empty. Only forty-five Scottish members of Parliament were to go and join the existing 513 in London, and the Scottish peers were to elect only sixteen of their members to join the House of Lords.

Dissatisfaction ran so high that several Scottish nobles presented themselves at St Germain and told the young king that it was now time for him to come over. It was exactly twenty years since his father had relinquished the Crown and James had spent all of his life, except for the first six months, in exile. He was a tall, distinguished young man with his father's aquiline nose and his mother's black eyes and hair. He had a natural reserve and, like his father, a distant manner, but no one could fault the painstaking way that he carried out his duties. The English exiles were justly proud of their king and even the fastidious French admired his intellectual accomplishments and his talents as a sportsman. His sister, Louise Marie, had all her mother's charm and her looks were much admired. It was even more galling, therefore, to realise that the insecurity of her position prevented her from being sought after as a bride and, though her mother had looked hopefully towards the French court, no offers had come forward.

James welcomed the Scottish envoys and was only too eager to answer his country's call, but, still cautious, Louis persuaded him to send Colonel Hooke on one more journey to Scotland to see how many nobles were finally able to commit themselves. The young king gave him the following command: "You are to repair to Scotland and to endeavour to meet with as many of our friends as you can to deliver to them our letters. You are to expose to them the necessity of laying hold of this opportunity of vindicating our right and their privilege and independency which if neglected may never be retrieved. As soon as they appear in arms and have declared for us we desire to come in person to their assistance." The final clause ran, "you are to assure each of our friends in particular of the true sense we have of his loyalty and sufferings on that account, which we think ourselves in honour and interest to reward to the utmost of our power."

Hooke again travelled in the north, where he knew that the main body of support lay. This time he met with more success. Feelings were running high and "there was scarce one in a thousand who did not declare for the king". It was generally felt that the country could not be in a worse state and any change might be for the better. Catholic Jacobites, Tory Jacobites and Covenanting Whigs were united in supporting the restoration of the young Stuart king. The Protestants were even prepared to pass over his Papism, "hoping God may convert him or he may have Protestant children". In Perthsire, Lord Stormont signed for the allegiance of seven supporters from the south. These included Nithsdale and Traquair. Lord Nithsdale, Hooke noted, was "Catholique and Puissant". He was unaware of the great difference that existed between clan chiefs in the north, who could call out hundreds of men at a nod, and the lairds in the south whose tenants made up their minds for themselves.

At last Louis was satisfied that sufficient support existed and, as he was being pressed hard on the battlefield by Marlborough in Flanders, anything that would divert the English would be to his advantage. To James's satisfaction he promised his support and began to assemble ships and arms at Dunkirk.

For a young man who had been brought up with only one ambition in mind, it was the fulfillment of a dream to be sent off at last to his own country, with the means to restore his family to the throne. He said farewell to his mother and sister, and with a group of English and Scottish supporters made for Dunkirk. However, no sooner had he arrived there than he developed a raging fever. He had caught measles from his sister and, when it was time to embark, he had to be carried onto the boat. Undeterred, he wrote a farewell note to his mother telling her that his next letter would be from Edinburgh Castle and the fleet set sail under the command of Admiral Comte de Forbin, who, in contrast to James, had reservations about the enterprise from the start.

They sailed into storms and violent seas and, after two ships had been lost, finally managed to cast anchor at the mouth of the Firth of Forth. There they lit fires and let off cannon and waited for an answer, but none came. The admiral became nervous and spying a ship in the distance he began to prepare for a retreat. James and his supporters on board begged him to stand firm saying that the boat that he saw was nothing more than a Danish merchant vessel which came to Edinburgh every year for pit-coal. They implored him to allow them to land, but he refused and an argument ensued between the admiral and James, who was desperate to set foot on Scottish soil. The admiral was adamant, saying that he could take no risks as he had been given full responsibility for James's safety. The quarrel was brought to a sudden close when it was confirmed that the so-called Danish coal ship was in fact an English naval vessel, arriving full tilt under the command of Admiral Byng. Nothing could stop de Forbin from making a hasty retreat, and the unfortunate James arrived back in France only three weeks after he had set out.

After it was over, the Jacobites agreed that they had lost one of the best chances that they were ever likely to have. The government had left Edinburgh virtually unarmed and the castle had been emptied and was without ammunition. Various reasons were put forward for the lack of success. (Communication had been at cross purposes, or the waiting ship's pilot had been drunk, among others) but on the whole the blame was put firmly on the French. Louis, they decided, had ordered de Forbin not to allow James to land, for he was more valuable to use as a pawn against the English than as an established king in his own kingdom. All he had wanted was a decoy to divert their attention.

Nevertheless the new English government had been given a fright. A proclamation from the queen was read out in Edinburgh. "We do hereby strictly command and require all good subjects to do their utmost endeavours to seize and apprehend the said

Pretender prince." In London, Roman Catholics were required to leave the city and to keep a distance of ten miles from it; all known Jacobite sympathisers were rounded up in Scotland, and William Nithsdale and Charles Traquair found themselves incarcerated in Edinburgh Castle.

James Francis Edward (engraving after Nicolas de Largilliere, Drambuie Collection).

Charles wrote a comforting letter to his wife. "I thought it would be agreeable to you to hear from myself that I thank God I am very well and the Castle air gives me a good stomach. We have very good company and liveth very pleasantly the only thing that troubles me is the want of you which though your health could allow you to come in you would not be allowed to stay here for none of our friends that have their Ladys in town can see them but with the greatest difficulty." Mary Traquair was at this time in her thirteenth confinement and about to give birth to a second pair of twins. The tone of his next letter had a more ominous note. "I long extremely my dearest to see you so if your health can allow I would have you take the opportunity of your mother's coach to come here. I thank God I am in perfect health and hath not been so well these several years as I have been since I came here wherefore I beg as you love me not to be discouraged for what else should happen to me. The bearer will inform you about what is to happen to all the prisoners."

Lord Nithsdale, Lord Traquair and the other six lords in the castle were required to give bonds varying from between three and five thousand pounds and then, on orders from London, were to be sent down to the capital under a strong guard. As a further humiliation London had decided that there was not a sufficient authority to examine them in Scotland. A contemporary observed, "and now it appeared to what a fine market Scotland had brought her hogs, her nobility and gentry being led in chains from one end of the island to the other merely on account of supposition and without any accusation or proof against them".

Mary Traquair went to stay with her mother and sister-in-law at Terregles before the prisoners left for London and her ten-year-old son, William Stuart, wrote to her in a childish hand: "Madam, That which is the greatest comfort to us all here is to hear that your ladyship and my Lord keep your health. We will all be in pain till we see your ladyship and my Lord come safely home, which I pray God may be soon. We are anxious to know likewise how my Lady Nithsdale keeps her health all my brother and sisters are in good health and offers their duty to your Ladyship and my Lord and beg your blessing and I myself Madam your Ladyship's most dutiful son and humble servant, William Stewart".

It was decided that Mary would return to Traquair with her mother and that Winifred would follow her husband down to London. Although, after a few months, the charges were dropped and they were allowed to return home, the prisoners had to bear the cost of the expedition themselves which added considerably to William's debts.

James's attempted landing had put the country on its guard against Catholics. Groups of soldiers were stationed throughout the country, stopping anyone on the road so Catholics began to attend mass either at night or in the very early hours of the morning. New Penal Laws were introduced whereby they were considered incapable of purchasing land or houses or of succeeding to inheritance. At the first Parliament after the Union they were also declared incapable of acquiring movables or of recovering just debts.

The Jesuit Bishop Gordon secretly made a tour of the Lowlands staying at Traquair where he confirmed some of the Stuart children and then going on to Terregles. Of all Scotland he found Nithsdale to be the most anti-Catholic part of the country. The people were so strongly Puritan that Catholics were regarded as heathens and idolators, and their houses were continually searched, while priests often had to spend the night in hiding out of doors. The Bishop's own visit was cut short when a local Minister led a riot against him while he was baptising a child.

In contrast to Mary Traquair's large family, the Nithsdales still had only one surviving child, their son William. Winifred had lost several children at birth or at an early age and was prone to miscarriages. She was never in robust health and the Jacobite Dr Archibald Pitcairn would ride out from Edinburgh to visit her and then if the weather allowed, continue on over the hills by Moffat to see the Traquairs. Dr Pitcairn was a man with wide interests and was full of good sense and learning: to celebrate the arrival of her first set of twins he had presented Mary Traquair with a four-lined verse in Latin. After Winifred's return from London she began to suffer from severe pains in her stomach. Her maids, alarmed, suggested that it might be an ulcer in her womb, and when she began to suffer from sleepless nights the devoted doctor was asked to visit. He soon diagnosed that she was suffering from a "felt gravel" which he convinced her was not serious and explained to her that the main cause of her weak condition was her fear that it might be something worse.

In 1710 both Winifred and Mary Traquair were "brought to bed". Winifred had a little girl Anne, who proved to be a healthy child and Mary had her sixteenth child, Robert, (though it seems that only seven of her children were still living).

The death of children was acceped with resignation and rarely mentioned and health was one of the main concerns of the time. Medicine was at such an early stage of development that one of the most most sought-after gifts was a successful cure. The following year Linton, Mary's eldest son, now thirteen, was taken ill and pleurisy was suspected. News of his sickness reached the Duchess of Gordon who heard that he had been "thrice blooded". She immediately dispatched the following prescripton which she claimed had "surprising success and which cannot possibly do any hurt". Mary was advised to go to "the house where the fouls stay and gather up carefully from the top of the hen's dung the white that lies above and make it in a powder, and give him as much as covers a halfpenny of this powder in any liquer your Ladyship thinks convenient, or my Lord Linton inclines most to drink of". The cure proved as beneficial as she claimed and Linton made a good recovery!

Old Lady Nithsdale was begining to fail in health and Winifred began to take over the management of the house. It was run with a small number of permanent servants who were given wages of a few pounds per annum (often unpaid at the end of one year and carried on till the next) but who received all their board and lodging and were also provided with their clothes. Laundry maids were employed on an ad hoc basis to deal with the vast quantities of table and bed linen, which was washed in a small washhouse built near a stream where a bleaching green had been made alongside. Butter, fresh and salted, and cheese were sometimes made in the dairy adjoining the house, the surplus being sold. At other times it was bought in from farms on the estate. Salmon, partridge, trout and chicken were all brought to the house by different individuals.

Occasional shopping expeditions were made to Edinburgh where Messrs Gordon in the Canongate supplied such items as grey paper (made in Penicuik), fine loaf sugar, cinnamon, ginger, soap, starch blue for washing, capers, vinegar, prunes, olives, anchovies, currants, mace and cloves. Candles were a large expense and both "cotton" and "ordinairy" were bought by the stone. Pottery and china were not yet in common use for tableware and pewter was used for many utensils. John Forbes, Pewterer, provided 45 pounds of dishes, stewpans, trenchers, chamber pots, pans, and a vinegar cruet, while old pewter items, which were taken in to be melted down were deducted from the bill.

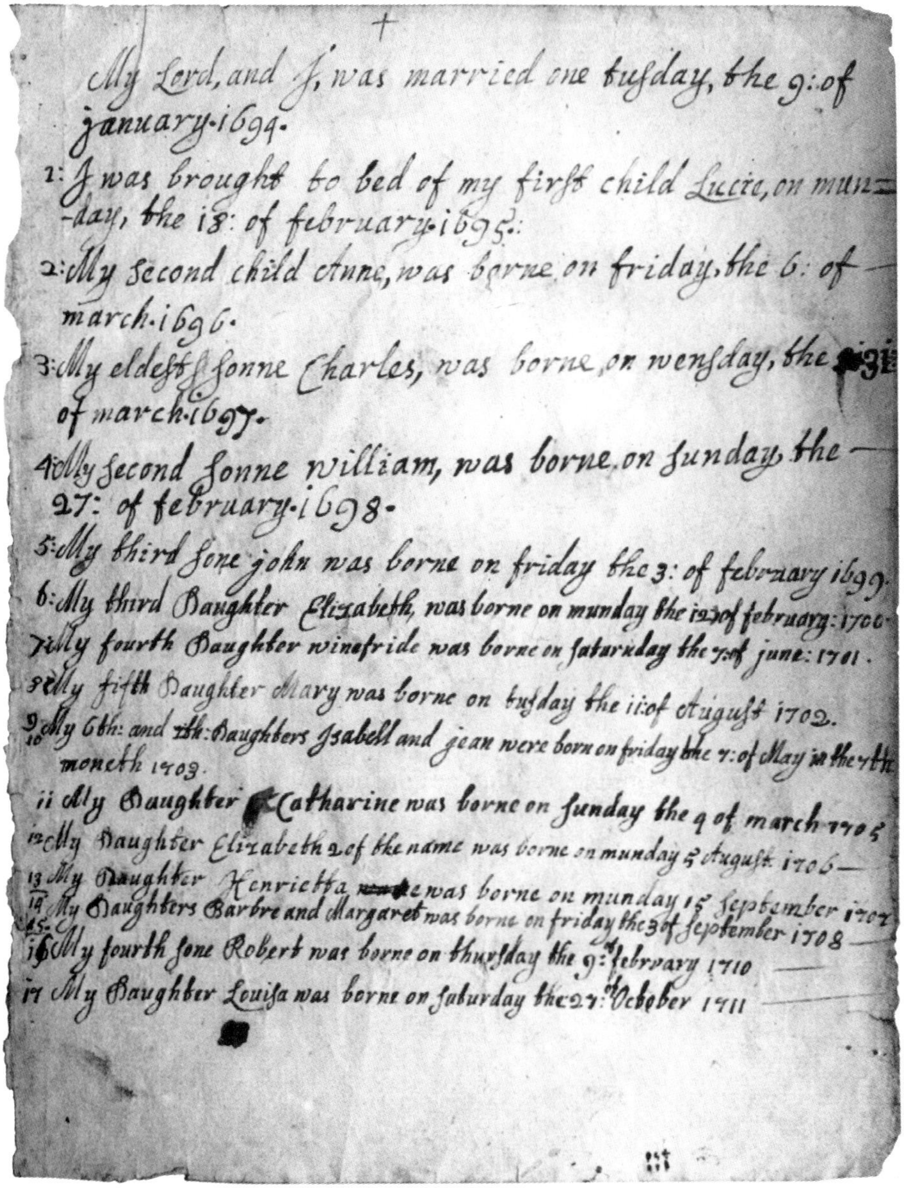

+
My Lord, and I, was married one tusday, the 9: of january 1694.
1: I was brought to bed of my first child Lucie, on mun-day, the 18: of february 1695:
2: My second child Anne, was borne on friday, the 6: of march 1696.
3: My eldest sonne Charles, was borne on wensday, the 31 of march 1697.
4 My second sonne william, was borne on sunday the 27: of february 1698.
5: My third sone john was borne on friday the 3: of february 1699.
6: My third daughter Elizabeth, was borne on munday the 12 of february: 1700.
7 My fourth daughter winefride was borne on saturday the 7 of june: 1701.
8 My fifth daughter Mary was borne on tusday the 11: of August 1702.
9 10 My 6th: and 7th: daughters Isabell and jean were born on friday the 7: of May in the 7th moneth 1703.
11 My daughter Catharine was borne on sunday the 4 of march 1705
12 My daughter Elizabeth 2 of the name was borne on munday 5 August 1706
13 My daughter Henrietta was borne on munday 15 september 1707
14 15 My daughters Barbre and Margaret was borne on friday the 3 of september 1708
16 My fourth sone Robert was borne on thursday the 9: february 1710
17 My daughter Louisa was borne on saturday the 27: October 1711

List of Lady Traquair's children in her own hand.

Winifred bought herself gowns, and petticoats, "mantoes" and stays, which were a vital part of the wardrobe and which were often taken back to be altered. In the winter she equipped herself with "wax" shoes to keep out the rain.

Like her sister-in-law Mary, who had laid out a parterre at Traquair, Winifred took a great interest in the garden. Over £40 worth of seeds were ordered each year, most of which were for the vegetable garden. A whole pound of onion seed was required for the year's cooking, half of which were "Strasburgh" and half "Flanders". Leek, carrot, parsnip, and cabbage were also needed in large quantities, while "pease" came in several kinds, "hotspur, haston, ruouervall, sugar or Turkish". Cucumber, "colliflower", gourd, melon and asparagus were well to the fore while hollyhock, sunflower, and French marigold sufficed for the flower border.

CHAPTER 8

Bankruptcy

James was determined not to be discouraged by the failure of his first attempt to regain his throne. He was young and had plenty of time. His adoring mother and sister Louisa Maria were waiting for him at St Germain with words of consolation and encouragement and in London Queen Anne was rapidly failing in health.

Anne still mourned the death of her husband, Prince George of Denmark, and the deaths of each of her children and she felt remorse for her disloyalty to her father. Perhaps to console herself she ate incessantly and was vastly overweight. The problem of her successor was a constant preoccupation and she considered her step-brother over the water infinitely preferable to her cousin Sophia's son, George of Hanover, who had in his youth rudely rejected her hand in marriage. His son, whom she had been forced to make Earl of Cambridge, she found even more unacceptable and she had refused to allow him to set foot in England. If only her tiresome step-brother would change his religion three kingdoms could be his for the asking.

But James was as fixed in his religion as she was in hers and, though he knew how easily he could have gained the Crown, he preferred to play a waiting game and felt sure he would eventually be king without having to compromise his beliefs. His followers constantly told him that, when that time came, his people would rise up in his support rather than accept his relation from Hanover.

In the meantime James joined the French army, calling himself the "Chevalier de St George". In the course of the war he found himself fighting at the Battle of Oudenarde against the combined armies of George of Hanover himself and the celebrated Duke of Marlborough who was so impressed by his courage on the battlefield that he enquired who the young soldier was and perhaps regretted that he had not persevered with his earlier overtures to the Jacobite side.

After the battle, James went to Bruges to visit Lucy in the Visitation Convent. It was a great day for the nuns and especially for Lucy, (now Sister Thérèse Joseph,) who had not seen the king since he was a child of four. The convent journal described every detail of the visit. James entered the enclosure with all his attendants, followed by a great crowd from the street. While he was there he "touched" several of the patients in the infirmary "in a devout and edifying manner though he was then but a young prince". The nuns had prepared a table with coffee, tea and assorted delicacies but he would take nothing as he had just come from dining with the French general, Comte de la Mothe. Before he left, the king also touched three of the nuns who were sick. The Stuart monarchs, with their profound faith in the divine right of kings, were great believers in touching for the King's Evil scrofula.

As James grew in stature and popularity, hope for the future sustained Mary Beatrice and the weary court at St Germain-en-Laye. But the unfortunate queen was to suffer further. Two years later, while James was visiting his family, he fell sick. The dreaded smallpox was diagnosed. While he lay in bed with a high fever, Louise Marie also fell ill and Mary Beatrice found herself with two children on the point of death. As James began to improve his sister's condition worsened until all hope was lost, and the captivating Louisa Maria died, aged eighteen, and was laid to rest beside her father.

Even the Sun king at Versailles was not immune to tragedy. Louis had already lost his eldest son, the Dauphin, earlier in the year when his eldest grandson, the Duc de Bourgogne, his charming wife Marie Adelaide, "the light of the court", and their five-year-old son, Louis, all died within twelve months of each other from the same ruthless disease. The following year the grieving Louis signed a Peace Treaty with England. In return for having his second grandson, the Duc d'Anjou, recognised as King of Spain, France was obliged to recognise the Hanoverian kings and to order the "Stuart Pretender" out of France. There was no alternative for James but to leave St Germain and accept the offer of hospitality from the Duke of Lorraine in Bar-le-Duc, taking many of the younger courtiers with him.

Back in Scotland the Nithsdales were virtually bankrupt. William's imprisonment in Edinburgh and the journey to London, all of which had to be paid for by the prisoners themselves, had been the last straw. William was advised by his lawyer that his only recourse was to make the whole of his estate over to his son, reserving only a life rent. Several Jacobite gentlemen were doing the same thing at this time only for a different reason: should they take up arms and find themselves on the losing side, their estates could not then be taken from them.

William enlisted the help of his brother-in-law Charles Traquair who reluctantly agreed to become a trustee. It was proposed that William should restrict himself to £500 a year until Charles and his other trustee, Maxwell of Munches, had managed to pay off all his debts. After the debts had been cleared the life rent from the estate would be transferred from William to his son who would then pay his father an allowance. At first William jibbed at this last clause: "I leave it to anyone to judge whether it is not more reasonable he should depend on me than I on him." However, he soon realised that there was no alternative. Just before the Trust was set up one of the creditors changed his mind and asked for his debt to be repaid in full. Munches asked Charles if he could raise £4000 to cover it but Charles refused, having made it quite clear from the beginning that he could not afford to support his brother-in-law. The Nithsdales were in a difficult position and Winifred, misunderstanding the situation, impetuously wrote to Charles saying that he had been "the ruin of her family". Charles patiently wrote back explaining the true situation, the creditor was appeased and the two families were able to maintain their good relationship as before.

The Traquairs had decided to send their two eldest daughters, Anne and Lucy away to school in France. So far they had been educated at home by the resident chaplain, with the rest of their brothers and sisters, but they needed "further advancement" in the arts of needlework, music, painting and dancing. It was also important for young ladies to learn French and to learn good English and English manners. Since the Union many of the Traquairs' and Nithsdales' friends and neighbours were travelling backwards and forwards to England where they had obtained government appointments. They were taking houses for the season in London instead of Edinburgh and some were sending their children to English schools. An English influence in the way of speech and dress was beginning to infiltrate north, and mothers who might have to extend their search for their daughters' husbands south did not want their girls to be looked upon as outmoded, with unfashionable clothes and Scottish accents. Good English could be learnt readily in France, since the convents were full of English ladies with a vocation, whose only alternative had been to enter a convent abroad.

The Ursuline convent in Paris was chosen for the girls. It had been recommended by the Duchess of Perth, who was still living at St Germain and was a friend of the reverend mother "Mrs" Waldergrave, as nuns were referred to. The two girls left Traquair in the autumn of 1713 and made the journey over to France in the safe hands of Mr Carnegie, a Catholic priest who acted as a liaison between Catholics in Scotland, the court of St Germain and the Nuncios in Paris.

The girls' parents waited eagerly for letters, which were usually brought home by the good offices of a priest or a friend. At first Lucy and Anne were homesick and missed Traquair and their large family. One of the nuns, Mrs Crichton, took them under her wing. She regarded the two new girls with dismay as she examined their meagre wardrobe and wrote back to their parents saying it was imperative that they should have a "woman to serve them who can dress well and learn them to do it". She stressed that "those far beneath their quality" employ a woman for this purpose. The girls themselves were made to feel like country bumpkins in comparison to the fashionable French girls who, as Lucy wrote, "are most unkind to us for which cause I will make all the haste I can to learn the French that I may get soon from amongst them". This meagre unfashionable wardrobe was a permanent embarrassment and it was a great relief when six months mourning was announced for the Duc de Berry, Louis' youngest grandson, who had died from injuries he had sustained in a hunting accident.

Queen Mary Beatrice invited the sisters to St Germain where she treated them with great kindness and refused to let them curtsy but embraced them instead. She asked them many questions about Scotland and told them that she remembered both of their grandmothers from the two sojourns that she and the king had spent at Holyrood when they were the Duke and Duchess of York.

By the following year the girls became more assured and began to receive visits from friends and relations from home. The Earl of Selkirk and the Marquis of Annandale called and invited them to the opera but they refused fearing that they would not be suitably dressed. Lucy confided to her mother that another gentleman had slipped a present of five guineas for each of them into her sleeve and she had not found it till she went to bed. He told them not to talk about it and said that he gave it because of the affection he held for their family. Gradually they became more interested in their dress and when their mother wrote to ask them what they would like sent over they asked for a "tolerable head to go out with". They had only one headdress each and would like to be able to ring the changes. They also wondered, as daughters do, whether she had finished with her silver clothes as they could be made into fine clothes for them to wear when they went out during the winter. It did not matter if there was not enough material for a whole outfit "as the French wear a manto of one thing and a petticoat of another." The following year they were confident enough to remove themselves to another convent where they were obliged to furnish their own rooms. They were sure, they told their parents, that they could resell the furniture when it was time to leave. As the costs mounted, Mary and Charles Traquair made up their minds that when the two boys went out in a few months' time with another priest, Mr Hall, the two girls should be brought home.

CHAPTER 9

George I

In 1714 Queen Anne lay dying in Kensington Palace, murmuring quietly to herself "my brother, my poor brother". Yet her preference for her successor was left unresolved. The Bishop of Oxford was heard to say at her deathbed, "Madam I will obey your commands. I'll declare your mind but it will cost me my head," but chose to keep his lips sealed. A packet found under her pillow was opened by Lord Bolingbroke, read and destroyed.

Immediately after her death, a Council of State was held in the palace and the Duke of Buckingham whispered to the Duke of Ormonde "My Lord you have twenty four hours to do our business and to make yourself master of the kingdom." A Hanoverian agent working in France stated openly that "the crown would belong to him who was first to seize it". Large areas of England were blatantly Jacobite, and since the Union, even more Scots purported to be on James's side.

James secretly left Bar-le-Duc and went to Paris to be ready to answer a call from his supporters at home, but none came. He had also hoped that more assistance would be forthcoming from France but Louis' military forces were severely reduced and this time he insisted that support should come from other quarters, namely his grandson, the King of Spain and the Pope. The French king was old and ailing, worn out by defeat on the battlefield and depressed by the mortalities in his family. Added to this, the strong-minded Madame de Maintenon was encouraging him to turn his eyes upwards towards the next world rather than attempt more gains in this one.

James's famous declaration to his loving subjects, stating that were fifty-seven persons nearer to the throne than George and setting out his own intention to get possession of "that right which is devolved upon us by the Laws of God and Man," was largely ignored.

George of Hanover arrived in London with a mistress on either side, leaving his wife locked up in a castle in Germany. He was greeted not only by Whigs but by many erstwhile Tory ministers and one of his first acts was to instruct the government to offer a reward of £100,000 "to seize and secure the Pretender in case he shall land or attempt to land in any one of his Majesty's Dominions".

The Jacobites did not shun his coronation, as Lady Cowper wrote in her diary, "they looked as cheerful as they could, but very peevish when anyone spoke to them". When the Bishop went round the throne demanding the consent of the people, Lady Dorchester, Catherine Sedley, James II's old mistress, might have muttered under her breath "does the old fool think that anybody will say no when there are so many drawn swords?" but was just as eager as all the other Stuart ex-mistresses and illegitimate offspring to take her place in the new court.

Back in Scotland, Catholic families were again being harassed by the Presbyterians who were full of renewed confidence now that there was a strong Protestant king on the throne. Catholics were advised to live as quietly as possible but their resolve to bring back a Catholic king grew stronger. By the following spring there were already signs that the Tory ministers who had offered their services to George and who had been rebuffed were anxious to transfer their allegiance to James. Ormonde and Bolingbroke were in touch with France and a two-fold invasion in the west of England and in Scotland was planned.

Charles Traquair decided that it was time for his two eldest sons, Charles, Lord Linton, and John Stuart, to complete their studies abroad at the Scots College in Paris. It would also be wise to get them out of the country should a rebellion take place. The Nithsdales, who were extremely fond of their nephews and nieces, made a special journey to Traquair to wish them goodbye.

The boys were accompanied by a priest, Mr Hall, as they travelled by stage-coach to London. From there they wrote their first letter home, full of excitement. They had by chance caught sight of the "King, Prince and Princess with the Turks and the rest of the court". Anxious to see the sights, they had visited the Tower and the recently rebuilt St Paul's Cathedral. Lord John Drummond had taken them to Kensington and the ring at Hyde Park, and Winifred's sister Frances Seaforth, had taken them to the playhouse. But they found everything "very deer" and bought only a few "stockens, cravats ruffles handkerchiefs and gloves".

The brothers left London for the coast in a hurry when it was discovered that Lord Bolingbroke had made the unfortunate mistake of sharing his mistress, Claudine de Tecin, with Cardinal Dubois, a well known Hanoverian spy. The result had been that all the Jacobite plans had been discovered, many of the plotters had been put in the Tower, and Bolingbrooke had made a dash for the coast before he was caught. Since the boys and their companion knew that all the boats would be stopped to prevent other conspirators from following him, they rushed to Dover to catch the last one. There, as Linton reported, they "met tygres rather than christians everyone striving who could cheat us the most". All three travellers were sick on the boat crossing the Channel and the company in the coach to Paris was "somewhat debauched for which Mr Hall was very pleased that we did not understand what was said".

The boys settled into the Scots College in Paris and had a joyful reunion with their sisters, now thoroughly at home in France and enjoying every minute of it. The news that they were to return home with Mr Carnegie, another priest who was leaving for

Scotland in a few weeks' time, was a bombshell. Letters went backwards and forwards between the girls and their parents and the unfortunate priest. Lucy pleaded that her "improvement" was not yet complete, that they had lost time at the Ursuline convent, being always ill, and that all the money that had been spent on their lessons up till now would be wasted if they returned with their education incomplete. Anne, Father Carnegie reported, was a little more amenable to returning than her sister but she was adamant that she would not return on her own so, "they must either stay together or go together". Worn out mentally trying to persuade the girls to abide by their parents' wishes, the unfortunate priest was also physically exhausted by the task of accompanying the four young people around the sights of Paris.

Now that Bolingbroke and Ormonde had been routed, new plans were being made. There was activity among Jacobites on both sides of the Channel and Father Carnegie was anxious to report back to Scotland, but still the girls procrastinated. He could stand it no longer and asked Lady Traquair to write to them with firm orders to return home. "I never was so weary of a place as I am of this", he complained.

But Lucy had one more card to play. She announced that she was thinking of becoming a nun and that this was her real reason for not wanting to leave the convent. She did not want to "expose herself to the temptations of the world". The priest wrote a long letter to Lady Traquair, addressing her by the pseudonym "Mrs Young", saying that he still felt that the best plan was to bring them home. He thought in this way Lady Lucy could "try if her vocation was from God, which if it be, her going home will rather confirm her in it than alter". The letter ended on a practical note, "if she desires back again your Ladyship will have the pleasure of seeing her before she leaves the world and the expenses of taking both home and sending her back again will be less than keeping both here for another year."

Having received a letter from Lady Traquair telling him to do whatever he thought best, the priest told the two young ladies to pack their trunks, engaged a Mrs Ramsay to accompany them, and booked places on the coach to Calais. As a concession, he promised them ten days in London to sightsee, and a visit to their cousin William Maxwell who was staying outside the town.

John Erskine, Earl of Mar (G. Kneller, National Galleries of Scotland).

CHAPTER 10

Mar raises Rebellion

With unshaken firmness and unconcealed political attachments they shook hands with ruin for what they esteemed the cause of their king and country.

BURNS

Although domestic life at Terregles and Traquair did not appear to have altered since they went away, the girls returned to Scotland at a crucial time and tension could be felt beneath the surface. One man had at last been prepared to throw down the gauntlet and lead a rebellion against the new Hanoverian king. John Erskine, 11th Earl of Mar, one of Queen Anne's ex-ministers, was an ambitious politician with a plausible manner. Known as "Bobbing John" for his ability to switch sides overnight, he owned large tracts of land in the north of Scotland and a house in Alloa where he had made outstanding gardens. Although in the past he had been instrumental in bringing about the Union and had acted against the Jacobites after the attempted rebellion in 1708, encouraging the Presbytery to hound Catholics on his estates, he now espoused the Jacobite cause with fervour and was hell-bent on leading a rebellion. It was galling for those who had been faithful to the Jacobite cause since its inception to find that this was the man who was to make himself leader of their party.

New plans had already been made for a landing in Scotland since those for the south had been abandoned. In May, William Nithsdale and other influential supporters in the south of Scotland, knowing that they were being watched by government spies, had met at Lochmaben under the cover of a race meeting. There, they had managed to drink the health of King James and form a Jacobite Association: since returning to their estates they had secretly been trying to gather together as many horses and arms as they were able in preparation for the coming fight.

The magistrates in the south west of Scotland were watching the situation carefully and, anxious to make a show of loyalty to the new king, they reported proudly to the Lord Provost, "we are advised that in Galloway and Nidsdaill a great many people are in readiness to show their zeal to H.M. King George being well armed and frequently rendezvouzing". The citizens of Glasgow sent an address to the new king, expressing their detestation for the "Popish Pretender".

At the beginning of August, the Earl of Mar secretly left London and travelled by boat to Newcastle and then on up to Elie in Fife. As he travelled through the country to his estates at Braemar he spread word that the government was about to introduce insupportable taxes on land, corn, cattle, meal, malt, horses, sheep and even cocks and hens. Since there was general discontent and distrust of the new government, his stories were readily believed. When he reached Braemar he sent out invitations to all of James's supporters to attend a "hunting party". Both William Nithsdale and Charles Traquair attended and, during the following days, Mar received frequent visits from Highland lairds and clan chiefs while Government spies kept a close watch on the proceedings, wrote down all they saw and sent their reports back to London.

On 27th August another "hunting party" was held, attended by 800 persons of all ranks. To disguise the purpose of the meeting, a real hunt took place by Glen Cluny and Glen Quoich. At the end of the day a magnificent brew of whisky, honey and boiling water was mixed in a vast hollow in the rock and offered as refreshment. Finally, on September 6th, King James's Standard, hastily sewn by the young Lady Mar, was raised. On one side were the arms of Scotland in gold and on the other a thistle and the motto "Nemo me impune lacessit". Below, on a background of blue silk, were stitched the words "no union". Two pendants proclaimed "for our wronged king and oppressed country" and "for ourselves and liberties".

After the raising of the Standard, Mar got up and spoke to the assembled company. He had the grace to first express his sorrow for his part in furthering the Union, and then announced that he had been empowered by James to be his Commander-in-Chief in Scotland, displaying, as proof, a Commission which he maintained had come from James. After assuring them that he had been promised sufficient money to launch the campaign and that arms, ammunition and men were soon to follow from France, he finished with the following cry: "now is the time for all good men to show their zeal for his Majesty's service, whose cause is so deeply concerned, and the relief of our Native Country from oppression and a foreign yolk too heavy for us and our posterity to bear, and to endeavour the restoring not only of our rightful king, but also our country to its ancient free and independent Constitution under him whose ancestors have reigned over us for so many generations." Those in the vicinity were exhorted to meet again in a few days' time with as many men, horses and arms as they could muster. Clan chiefs were expected to bring out all their men. This was one of their prerogatives, and at the "burning of the heather", each man in the clan was supposed to leave whatever he was doing and rally at once to his chief's call.

Mar was a persuasive speaker but, knowing his past record, not everyone was convinced. There were doubts that he had actually been empowered by James and about the authenticity of his Commission.

A few days later Mar had his address printed in Edinburgh and circulated to the nation. In it he promised that "every officer who joins us in our King and Country's cause shall not only enjoy the same post he now does, but shall be advanced and preferred according to his rank and station and the number of men he brings with him to us". The amount of pay that would be received by each man was also advertised.

In London, the government was nervous and passed an Act for Encouraging Loyalty. This invited "suspected persons whose estates or principal residence are in Scotland to appear in Edinburgh or where it shall be judged expedient, to find bail for their good behaviour".

Both Charles and William received this invitation and both declined it. Only two people did respond and they were immediately clapped into Edinburgh Castle, while those who did not answer the summons became officially outlaws, and liable to be picked up at any time. The two brothers-in-law had to decide what part they would play in the forthcoming rebellion. In the event the decision was taken that William would risk his all, "come out" and join the army in the south of Scotland but that Charles Traquair would stay at home. There were good reasons to support both men's decision.

It was a well known ploy for two relations to take different sides, so that one family would not suffer complete annihilation. William was the obvious one to take the risk. He was almost bankrupt, and his estate had been made over to his son. The south west of Scotland, where he lived, was an intensely Whig and anti-Jacobite and anti-Catholic area, and his life was becoming intolerable. His son had already had to leave home and now he only had his small daughter Anne. Though nearly forty, he was younger than Charles Traquair and furthermore his wife, Winifred, brought up in the exiled court, was a fervent Jacobite supporter and ready to take all the risks involved.

Charles on the other hand was a man in his mid fifties and had been in poor health for some time. He was devoted to his wife and large family and did not wish to risk leaving them on their own. He had, in any case, already been imprisoned twice for the Jacobite cause. He was also a prudent man and, having assessed Mar's capabilities as a general, may well have realised they were not of the highest calibre.

Many families found themselves split in two at this time, for in the same family some members were Jacobites while others supported King George. The vast majority, it must be said, preferred not to be involved at all and were not particularly interested in who sat upon the throne in faraway London.

Mar began to advance southwards, his army gaining strength as it went. Like a great snowball, the larger it became, the more men came out to join him and the lords in the south listened with excitement as messengers brought news first of the capture of Perth, then Kirkcaldy, Kinghorn, Dysart and all the towns on the north side of the Forth. Finally the whole of the kingdom of Fife, Forfar, Kincardine, Aberdeen, Banff and Moray, as well as Perth and Inverness, had come under the Jacobite standard. An attempt to take Edinburgh Castle had only just been foiled and it was expected daily that James would arrive with the much needed men and arms from France.

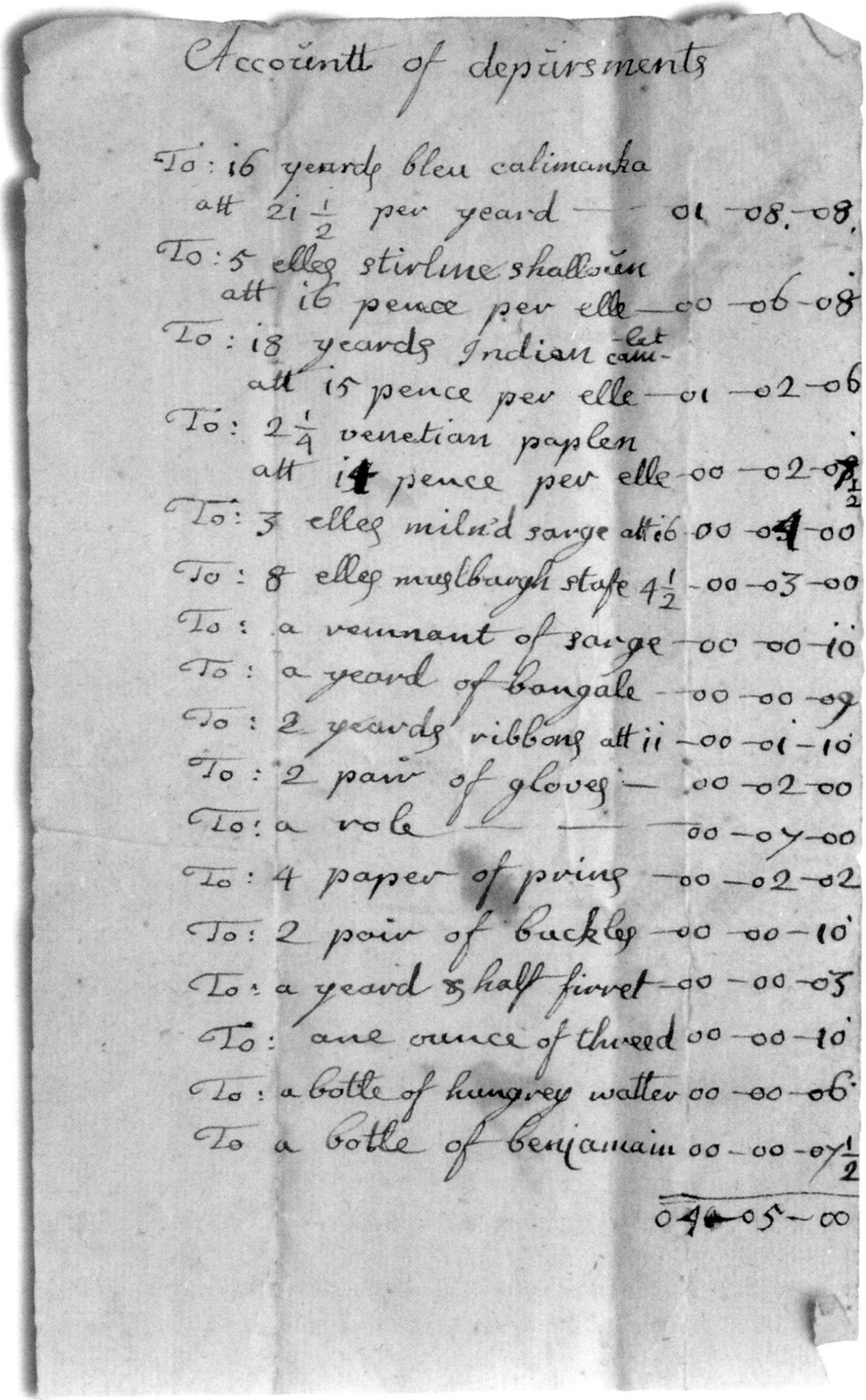
Accountt of depursments

To: 16 yeards bleu calimanka
att 21 1/2 per yeard — 01-08-08
To: 5 elles stirline shalloun
att 16 pence per elle — 00-06-08
To: 18 yeards Indian camlet
att 15 pence per elle — 01-02-06
To: 2 1/4 venetian paplen
att 14 pence per elle — 00-02-07 1/2
To: 3 elles miln'd sarge att 16 — 00-04-00
To: 8 elles muslbaurgh stafe 4 1/2 — 00-03-00
To: a remnant of sarge — 00-00-10
To: a yeard of bangale — 00-00-09
To: 2 yeards ribbons att 11 — 00-01-10
To: 2 pair of gloves — 00-02-00
To: a role — 00-07-00
To: 4 paper of pins — 00-02-02
To: 2 pair of buckles — 00-00-10
To: a yeard & half fivret — 00-00-03
To: ane ounce of threed 00-00-10
To: a botle of hungrey watter 00-00-06
To a botle of benjamain 00-00-07 1/2

04-05-00

CHAPTER 11

Defeat at Preston

Wigton's coming, Nithsdale's coming,
Carnwath's coming, Kenmure's coming,
Derwentwater and Forster's coming,
Withrington and Nairn's coming-
Little what ye wa's coming-
Blythe Cowhill and a's coming.

At the beginning of September Mar's army appeared to be unbeatable. The government, who had been prepared for a rebellion but uncertain where it would start, sent the Duke of Argyll to take command of the government troops in Scotland. They found themselves completely outnumbered. By mid-September Argyll had only 1400 men against what he (over)-estimated to be 10,000 Jacobites. He wrote urgently from Edinburgh to Lord Townsend that without considerable reinforcements or a miracle, "not only this country will be utterly destroyed but the rest of his Majesty's dominions put in the extremest danger". By the end of the month Mar had in fact, accumulated an army of between four and five thousand men and had set up his camp at Perth. Here his incompetence as a military leader was revealed, for instead of taking the initiative and overpowering Argyll's meagre forces, he decided to wait. Neither did he use this time to organise his army even in the matter of basic arrangements of food and lodging. Weapons and ammunition were scarce and he made no effort to obtain more. The renowned maxim to "keep your powder dry" was also neglected for, as they had no powder horns, the men were obliged to keep their powder in their pockets and it often became too wet to use. Waiting was totally against the Highland character and they soon became bored and mutinied for more pay, or decided to return home until they were needed.

One excuse Mar had for his lack of action was the fact that he did not know when or where James would arrive with the much needed men and arms from France. It was known that Louis had finally agreed to send help and that twelve large ships with 2000 men, weapons and ammunition lay at Havre de Grace ready to embark for Scotland, and it was generally expected that they would land at Dumbarton.

At the end of September disaster struck. Their loyal supporter, King Louis XIV died, leaving his four-year-old great-grandson as his heir. The boy's great-uncle, the Duc d'Orleans, who was appointed Regent, was more interested in keeping on good terms with George I than befriending the Jacobites. He was immediately leant upon by Lord

Stair, the British ambassador in Paris, to order the larger ships to be unloaded. Thus James's departure was further delayed.

William Nithsdale and the lowland lords decided that it was time to assemble their men with the idea of meeting up with the Jacobite forces in the north of England. It was arranged that William Nithsdale, Lord Kenmure and Lord Carnwarth should start by meeting at Moffat and should challenge the loyal forces there. Lord Kenmure, a landowner in Kirkcudbrightshire and an Episcopalian Tory, had reluctantly accepted a commission from James to command the troops in the south of Scotland. It had been thought wise to give the leadership to the High Church Tories in order to persuade the rest of them to "come out".

William bade Winifred goodbye and, accompanied by a handful of tenants and personal servants who had agreed to join him, set off from Terregles for the small border town of Moffat where Kenmure and Carnwarth were waiting. A few bystanders watched, without protest, as they raised King James's Standard at the Market Cross. Having made this successful start, they decided, with great bravado, to move on to Dumfries and take the town. On their way they were further encouraged by taking possession of seventeen stands of arms which had been deposited at the house of a local Whig.

Before they reached Dumfries, a messenger came to warn them that the town had armed itself and was waiting for them. Their enthusiasm quickly diminished, and they decided instead to play a cautious game and make for the smaller town of Ecclefechan. From there they marched to Langholm, which had already surrendered to Lord Wintoun, the eccentric peer from East Lothian who was not such a fool as he liked to pretend. This wild young man had managed to bring a large number of men with him and together they now numbered 180. They divided themselves into two squadrons, one under Lord Wintoun and one under Lord Carnwarth.

The question was, where to go next. Information from Mar in the north and from the rising in Northumberland was slow to reach them and they were at a loss to know how they fitted into Mar's plan, or if in fact he had one. When they heard that the English Jacobites were meeting at Rothbury they decided that they should make the four-day journey to join them. By the time they arrived it was dark, but the English had successfully taken the town and were camping in fields outside.

The Scots met the English leaders, Lord Derwentwater, a young Catholic from Northumberland whose mother had been a mistress of Charles II, and Tom Foster, a Member of Parliament, in the Old Black Bull. The English Jacobites were in low spirits. They had failed to take Newcastle and, as they knew that they were being watched, had been unable to signal back to a French ship which had been waiting to land with the supplies that they were so badly in need of. They had been obliged to watch her sail away without unloading.

The next morning, in daylight, the Scots looked at the English army with scorn. They were mounted on blood horses as if ready for a day's hunting and few had war saddles or arms of any kind. While the English were surprised by the Scots, whose mounts were rough and ready, but who were well armed, with basket-hilted broadswords. Although no instructions had been received from Mar a messenger reported that "Old Borlum", Brigadier Mackintosh, was on his way south with a force of 2000 men. He had daringly outwitted the government troops, had crossed the Firth of Forth under the noses of their men-of-war, and had even attempted an attack on Edinburgh on the way. It was decided to travel north again and meet him at Kelso.

On Sunday 23rd October, soaked to the skin after marching through heavy rain, they waited in the square at Kelso as, to the skirl of pipes, Old Borlum and his Highlanders, equally drenched and mud-spattered, marched proudly into the town. A service was held in the kirk which was packed to capacity, and a manifesto was read deploring the Union and expressing the hope that King James would "lose the prejudices attributed to his education in a foreign country". The combined army was now divided into five troops. To prevent discord, the curious arrangement was made that Kenmure would be the commander in Scotland and, if they crossed the border into England, Foster would take over.

While they were discussing where they should go next, a messenger arrived from Mar. His letter started with the cheerful hope that "if we do not mismanage I think our game can scarce fail," but gave little instruction as to how the next move should be played. He himself was waiting in Perth for the arrival of forces from the north and they were to do whatever they thought best.

They had to make up their minds quickly. A report was received that General Carpenter was approaching fast with government forces from the south. The English were anxious to return to their own country and the Highlanders were determined not to set foot in England. As a compromise, it was decided to march along the wet, boggy line of the border to Jedburgh and Hawick and finally, two weeks later, they ended up where they had started, in Langholm.

Here another argument ensued. The English were more determined than ever that they should go south and join up with the large number of High Church Tories who they were sure were waiting to meet them. Wintoun, who knew the mind of his men, and the old warrior, Borlum, were both opposed to this and would have preferred an engagement with the government army but eventually they were forced to give in. Nevertheless 500 Highlanders refused on any account to cross the Border and decided to return home. The majority were captured in Lanarkshire.

The rest of the army marched south via Penrith and Appleby and on to Kendal. At each town James III was proclaimed and the money from the Excise Office and Customs

House was appropriated. At Doncaster they were met by Lord Widdrington who brought encouraging reports of support further south. But as they continued on their way they became depressed by the small number of men who came out to join them.

A few days later they reached Preston and were heartened to hear that the news of their approach had caused two government dragoons to leave the town. The local Catholic gentry, who had been more eager to toast the king over the water than actually come out and risk their lives for him, exonerated their guilt by extending liberal hospitality. The leaders, feeling secure and ready for a rest, decided to linger for a second night so that the whole army could take a short leave.

The following morning, a messenger brought the disturbing news that government troops were approaching fast from the south and were already within a few miles of the town. The Jacobite leaders held a hasty meeting and decided not to hold the Ribble bridge but to barricade themselves into the town instead. They did this successfully enough to stand up to the first onslaught, but when General Carpenter arrived with reinforcements, all the exits to the town were blocked. The Jacobites had only two choices, either to surrender or to fight their way out. Borlum and his Highlanders, together with Wintoun, favoured the latter but the English and Borderers, aware of the high mortality this would entail, chose surrender.

General Wills, the Government general, offered to protect the Jacobites if they surrendered as "prisoners of discretion as rebels taken in the act of rebellion" and gave them an hour to decide. The Jacobites asked for more time but by 7 a.m. on Monday 14th November they acquiesced. The terms they had been offered were the worst possible and denied them all rights.

The Jacobite officers were ordered to hand over their swords in the churchyard, while the lords were allowed to go to the Mitre Inn to carry out this humiliating procedure in private. They were then put under guard in various inns about the town while the men were shut, unfed, into cold, damp churches. There they remained for several days while a court martial was held for the regular officers, four of whom were shot the following day.

The prisoners were divided up and Lord Nithsdale and the six peers were put in a carriage and, under the escort of Stanhope's Dragoons, taken to Wigan en route for London. Behind them rode the prisoners of lesser rank. They stopped at Middlewatch where William was able to send a hurried letter to Winifred assuring her that he was well but, as usual, had no money. He asked her to send some by messenger to Barnet, which they were supposed to reach by 10th December and then to prepare herself to come to London. He had heard they would be made "close" prisoners and he would have no one to petition for his release and would have no contact outside.

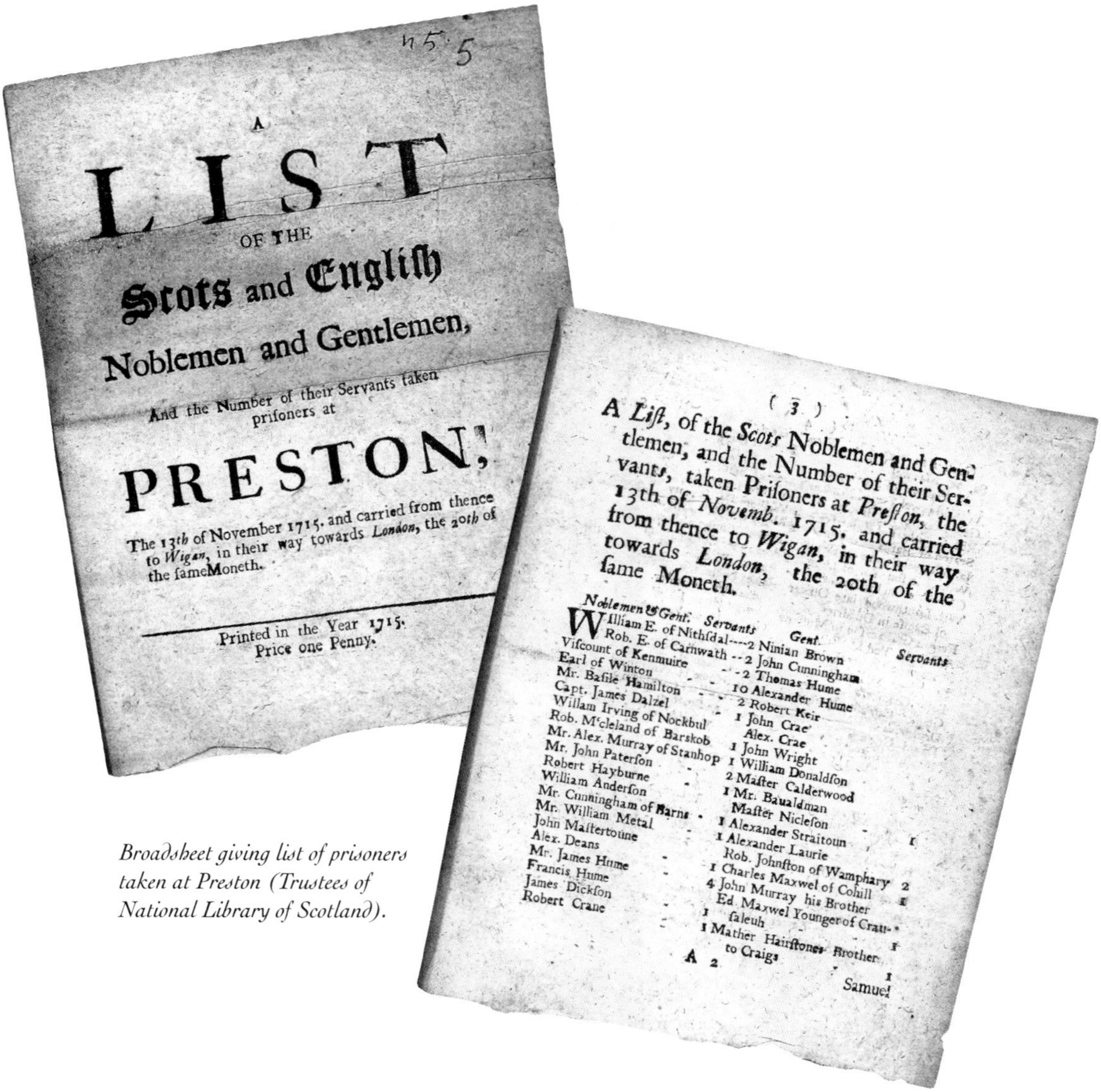
A
LIST
OF THE
Scots and English
Noblemen and Gentlemen,
And the Number of their Servants taken
prisoners at
PRESTON,
The 13th of November 1715. and carried from thence
to Wigan, in their way towards London, the 20th of
the same Moneth.

Printed in the Year 1715.
Price one Penny.

(3)
A List, of the Scots Noblemen and Gentlemen, and the Number of their Servants, taken Prisoners at Preston, the 13th of Novemb. 1715. and carried from thence to Wigan, in their way towards London, the 20th of the same Moneth.

Noblemen & Gent. Servants Gent. Servants
William E. of Nithsdal----2 Ninian Brown
Rob. E. of Carnwath --2 John Cunningham
Viscount of Kenmuire --2 Thomas Hume
Earl of Winton - - 10 Alexander Hume
Mr. Basile Hamilton - - - 2 Robert Keir
Capt. James Dalzel - 1 John Crae
William Irving of Nockbul Alex. Crae
Rob. M'cleland of Barskob 1 John Wright
Mr. Alex. Murray of Stanhop 1 William Donaldson
Mr. John Paterson - 2 Master Calderwood
Robert Hayburne - 1 Mr. Baualdman
William Anderson - Master Nicleson -
Mr. Cunningham of Barns - 1 Alexander Straitoun 1
Mr. William Metal - 1 Alexander Laurie
John Mastertoune Rob. Johnston of Wamphary 2
Alex. Deans - 1 Charles Maxwel of Cohill 1
Mr. James Hume - 4 John Murray his Brother
Francis Hume - Ed. Maxwel Younger of Crautaleuh
James Dickson - 1 -
Robert Crane - 1 Mather Hairstones Brother to Craigs 1
A 2 1
Samuel

Broadsheet giving list of prisoners taken at Preston (Trustees of National Library of Scotland).

They reached Barnet two days earlier than expected and got to Highgate on the 9th December. Here preparations were made for their entry into London, for the government was determined to make a public exhibition of them. William, like the rest of his peers, was given a horse to mount, his arms were tied tightly behind his back and the reins were taken by a soldier on foot. Like trussed chickens they were led through the city while the General's drums beat a victorious march. Crowds lined the streets to watch their humiliation, jeering and banging on warming-pans, and shouting, "King George for ever, no warming pan bastard". Lady Cowper, wife of the Lord Chancellor and a dedicated Whig, was so disgusted by this degrading spectacle that she refused to watch and would not let her children do so.

At the centre of the town the prisoners were again divided up. William and his fellow peers were sent to the Tower, those of slightly lower rank were sent to Newgate, and the remainder to the prisons of Marshalsea and the Fleet. William Nithsdale, for extra security, was placed in the Lodgings of the Lieutenant Governor.

CHAPTER 12

To London

Green Nithsdale, make moan for they leaf's in the fa',
The lealest of they warriors are drapping awa';
The rose in they bonnet, that flourished sae and shone,
Has lost its white hue, and is faded and gone.

All this time Winifred had been waiting anxiously at Terregles for news of William. When his letter was brought to her, she immediately rode over to Traquair and sought Charles's advice. Charles himself was keeping a low profile for, since he had not answered his summons to Edinburgh, he knew he might be arrested at any time.

Rumours of the defeat at Preston had already come to their ears and they had also heard that, on the very same day, Mar had taken on the government troops at Sherriffmuir. Although the Jacobites had outnumbered their opponents by more than three to one, lack of military expertise had left the outcome indecisive and there were heavy losses on both sides. After the battle many of the Highlanders had decided to return home to see their families and Jacobite morale was low. Inverness was won back by Lord Lovat and Mar abandoned his intention to march south. All hopes rested on the arrival of James, who still had not been able to leave France.

The Traquairs were anxious to do everything in their power to help and, realising that Winifred was determined to make the journey to London, advised her to dismiss all the servants and to close up her house before she left. Charles, knowing the cost of living in the Tower and the expense of a lawyer to plead William's case, lent her as much as he could spare. The Traquairs arranged to collect little Anne and her nurse, Mrs Lindsay, and promised to look after her in Winifred's absence. Winifred followed their instructions, only keeping on in her employment the "grieve" and the "byre woman." She also arranged for the gardener's wife to light fires in the house to keep it from getting damp, for winter was coming on and all the signs were that it would be a severe one. Maxwell of Cruachan agreed to oversee the estate but to take no action without further orders.

It was too late to send the money to William at Barnet as he had requested so she was anxious to leave as soon as possible, taking with her what she could. As always, money was in short supply but their Edinburgh lawyer, William Alves, moved by her plight, supplemented the amount he could give her with a loan of £100 of his own.

Her last action was carried out at night. With her trusted gardener she walked to the end of the wide, grassed-over terrace which lay at the back of the house. There she ordered him to cut through the frozen turfs and dig a deep hole. Into it she placed the documents dealing with the transfer of the estates to her son, and the grass was carefully replaced, scarcely leaving a mark.

Cecilia Evans was to be her companion on the long journey south and the next day Winifred and Evans made themselves ready for the journey. The ground was frozen hard and they wrapped themselves in many layers of clothing, trying to look as unremarkable as possible. They planned to travel by horseback to Newcastle and, from there, to catch the London coach. To avoid Dumfries and Carlisle, which were by now full of government troops, they made their way across the snow-covered countryside, spending the night at small inns on the way. The severe weather had driven everyone to their firesides and they met with few strangers in those isolated parts. After travelling for five days, they arrived at Newcastle on 15th December and immediately went to book places on the London coach, but discovered that all the places had been taken. Reluctant to wait several days for the next coach, Winifred decided that they should ride on to York and try to get places on the London coach from there. A gentleman in the same predicament took pity on them and, knowing that he would get to York quicker than they would, promised to keep them places if they were available. If there were none, Winifred asked him to hire horses as she was now desperate enough to ride all the way to London if necessary.

On their arrival at York they found that the kind stranger had been as good as his word and had booked the last available seat on the coach for Winifred and hired a horse for Evans. As they set off a blizzard set in; the snow began to thicken and gather in great drifts and they were forced to make frequent stops while the coachman and passengers got out to dig the wheels out of the snow. Progress was slow and they were only able to travel in fits and starts for the next two and a half days. There was no let up in the weather and, sixteen miles north of Grantham, the coach stuck in a drift and came to a permanent halt. The passengers were forced to abandon it and make for the nearest inn. Winifred, frantic to get to William as soon as possible, refused to join them but insisted on hiring a horse for herself and a fresh one for Evans and together they managed to ride on through the blizzard.

On Christmas Day she wrote from Stamford to Mary Traquair. "The snow was so deep that our horses yesterday was in several places almost buried in the snow. I must confess such a journey I believe was scarce ever made, considering the weather, by a woman. But an earnest desire compasses a great deale, with God's help; and I may say that the delayes and stops I have unavoidably met with to my more speedy performance of it, have been by far the greatest difficulty I have had, though if I had known what I was to have gone through, I should have doubted whether I was able to have done it." She thanked her for looking after her "little girl" and added "had I had her with me she would have been in her grave by this time with the excessive cold".

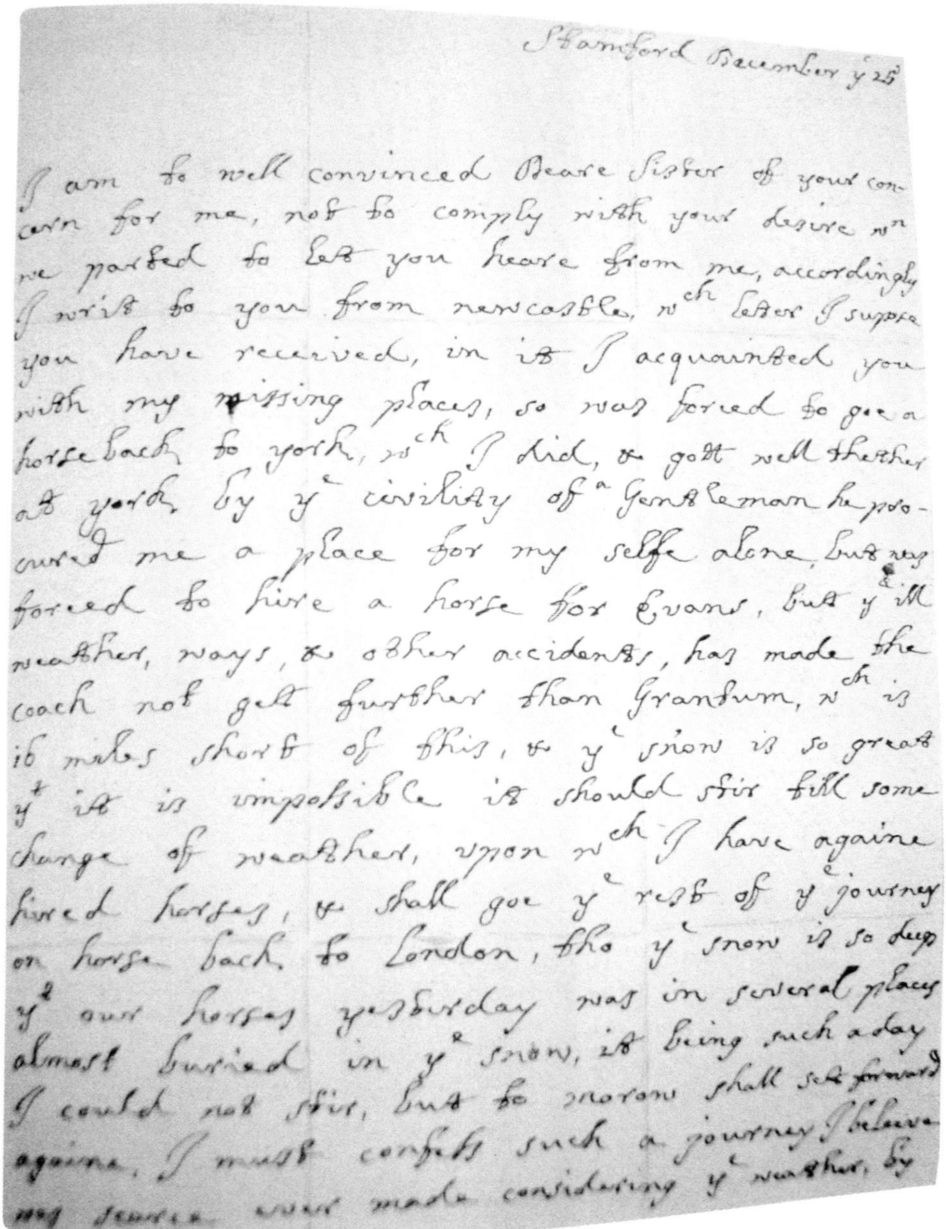
Stamford December ye 25

I am so well convinced Deare Sister of your con-
cern for me, not to comply with your desire wn
we parted to let you heare from me, accordingly
I writ to you from newcastle, wch letter I suppose
you have received, in it I acquainted you
with my missing places, so was forced to goe a
horse back to york, wch I did, & gott well thether
at york by ye civility of a Gentleman he pro-
cured me a place for my selfe alone, but was
forced to hire a horse for Evans, but ye ill
weather, ways, & other accidents, has made the
coach not gett further than Grantum, wch is
16 miles short of this, & ye snow is so great
yt it is impossible it should stir till some
change of weather, upon wch I have againe
hired horses, & shall goe ye rest of ye journey
on horse back to London, tho ye snow is so deep
yt our horses yesterday was in several places
almost buried in ye snow, it being such a day
I could not stir, but to morow shall set forward
againe, I must confess such a journey I believe
was scarce ever made considering ye weather, by

Lady Nithsdale's letter from Stamford.

When they finally arrived in London they went straight to their old friend Mrs Mills in Duke Street where they knew they would always be welcome. Winifred was in a pitiable state after her journey, racked with exhaustion and running a fever, but nothing would prevent her from making her way to the Tower. Through judicious bribery she was allowed a short visit with her husband.

William was living in solitary confinement on the second floor of the Lieutenant's Lodgings, well guarded by warders. He told her that on the day after their arrival in London he and the other six peers had been examined by the Lords of Council. They had also been impeached in the House of Commons for High Treason and brought before the Bar of the House of Lords, charged with the Articles and asked to give in their answers. Sentence was due on the 9th February.

William and his fellow prisoners had been advised by their lawyers to plead guilty, claiming that they had acted upon the principles of conscience and were ready to undergo any penalty allotted to them. To this the Earl of Carnwarth had muttered that "now he had been led about like a dog on a string, they might e'en dispatch him which ever way they pleased".

William was in a pessimistic mood. It was a bitter irony to learn that, after Mar had lost half his army after the Battle of Sheriffmuir, and while the Jacobites taken at Preston lay in their various prisons, James had at last managed to cross the sea and land at Peterhead in the north of Scotland. However, his sojourn in his "own and ancient kingdom" had lasted less than five weeks and had been a dismal failure. James had been disheartened to find that the rebellion for which he had waited all his life had collapsed before his arrival. Added to that, the extreme Scottish winter had caused him to fall ill with ague.

The Scots, already despondent, felt that their king did not match their expectations. His reserved manner and his apathy, due to his illness, did not inspire them. After an abortive attempt to rally the Jacobite troops once more, and a pitiable crowning ceremony at Scone, James was persuaded that better terms of surrender would be obtained for the prisoners without his presence. So, on February 4th, he bade his followers farewell and sailed back to France, the ubiquitous Earl of Mar at his side.

The arrival and departure of James was actually detrimental to the Jacobite lords. On January 21st King George had addressed Parliament and referred to the landing of the "Old Pretender". The reply of the two Houses declared that "the landing of the Pretender hath increased their indignation against him and his adherents and they were determined to do everything in their power to assist His Majesty, not only in subduing the present rebellion, but in destroying the seeds and causes of it that the like disturbance may never rise again to impair the blessings of His Majesty's reign".

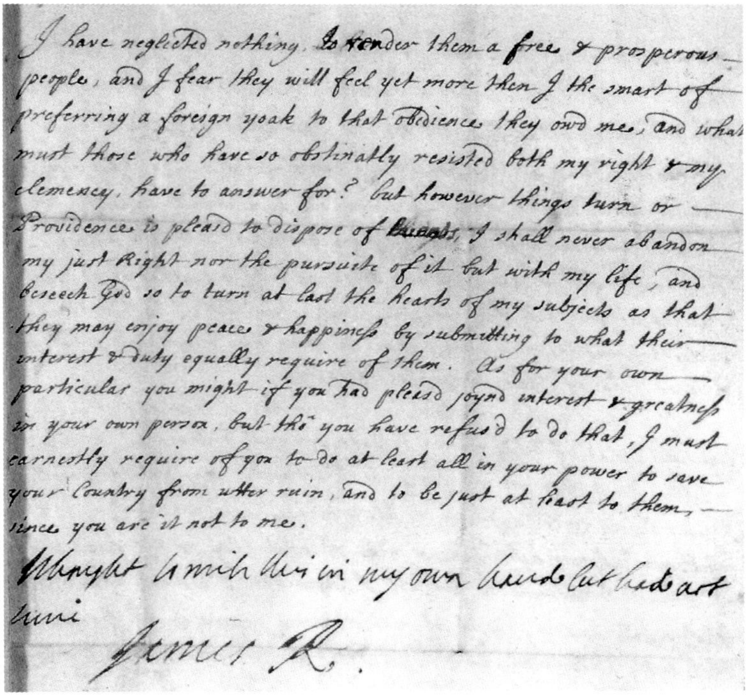

I have neglected nothing to render them a free & prosperous people, and I fear they will feel yet more then I the smart of preferring a foreign yoak to that obedience they owd me, and what must those who have so obstinatly resisted both my right & my clemency, have to answer for? but however things turn or Providence is pleas'd to dispose of [illegible], I shall never abandon my just Right nor the pursuite of it but with my life, and beseech God so to turn at last the hearts of my subjects as that they may enjoy peace & happiness by submitting to what their interest & duty equally require of them. As for your own particular you might if you had pleas'd joyn'd interest & greatness in your own person, but tho' you have refus'd to do that, I must earnestly require of you to do at least all in your power to save your Country from utter ruin, and to be just at least to them, since you are it not to me.

I thought to write this in my own hand but had not time

James R.

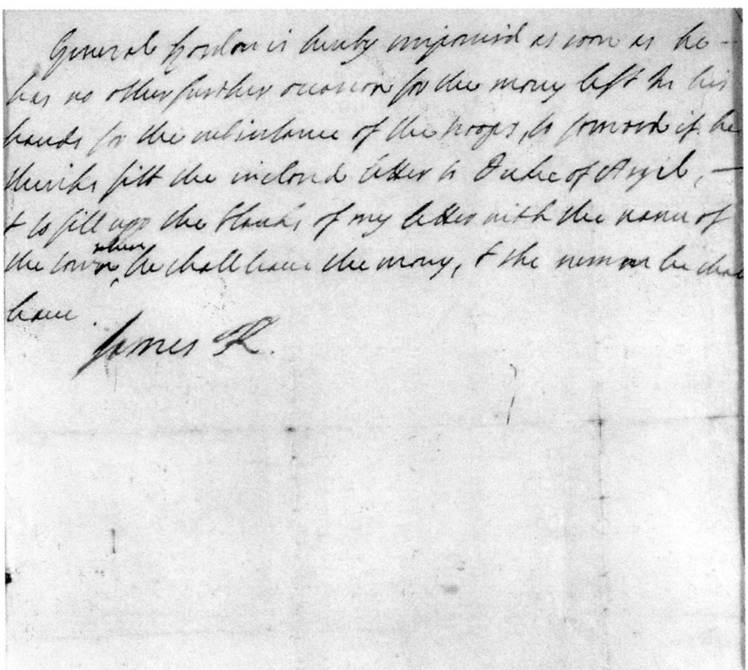

General Gordon is hereby impowred as soon as he has no other further occasion for the mony left in his hands for the subsistance of the troops, to forward if he thinks fitt the inclosed letter to Duke of Argyl, & to fill upp the blanks of my letters with the name of the town where he shall have the mony, & the number he shall have.

James R.

Letter written by James Edward Stuart after retreat from Perth (Drambuie Collection).

After visiting William, Winifred returned to Duke Street and became so ill with exhaustion and sickness that she was forced to take to her bed. As she wrote again to Mary Traquair, "all the comfort I had in it was that, all the while I lay ill, had I been otherwise, nothing could be done for my Lord during that time, nor can yett, till after next Thursday, when 'tis supposed sentence will be past against them. God Almighty help us, and send us success."

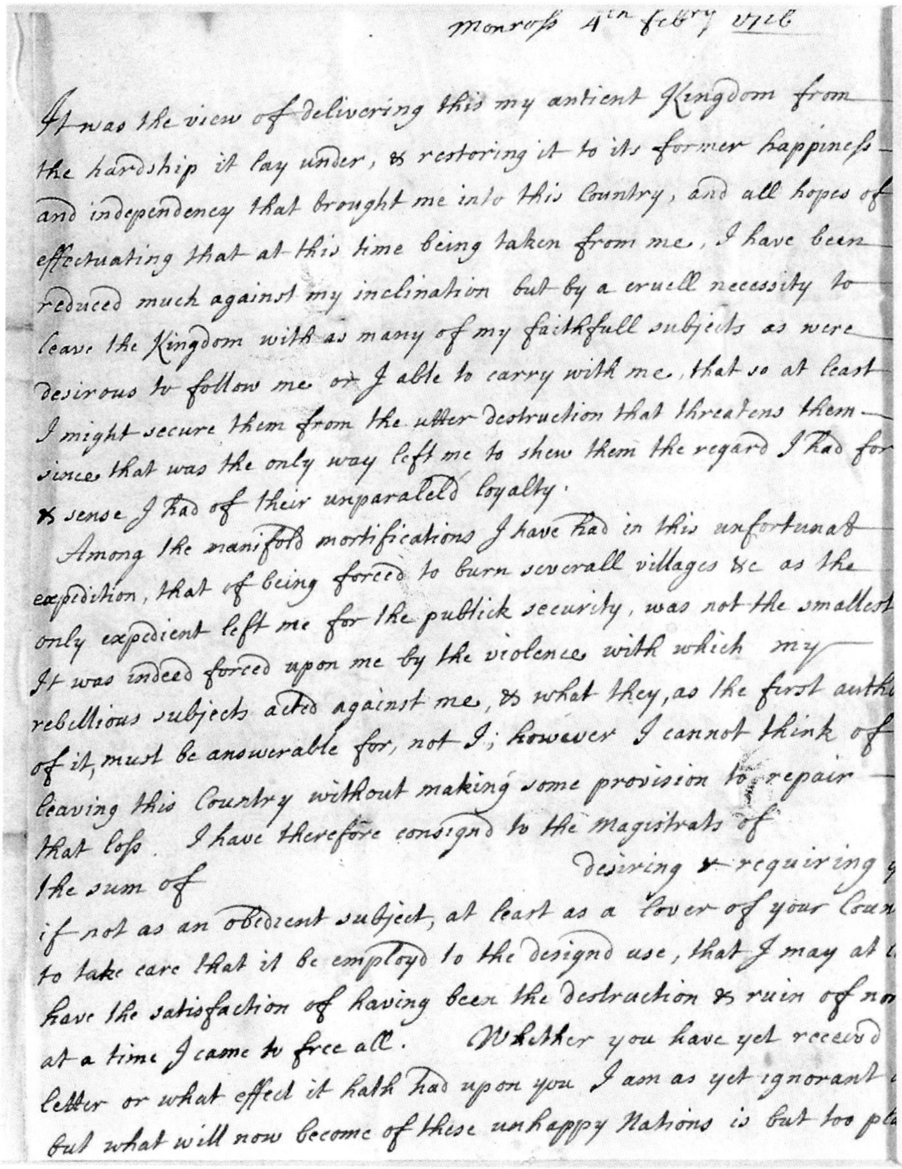
Monross 4th feb'ry 1716

It was the view of delivering this my antient Kingdom from
the hardship it lay under, & restoring it to its former happiness
and independency that brought me into this Country, and all hopes of
effectuating that at this time being taken from me, I have been
reduced much against my inclination but by a cruell necessity to
leave the Kingdom with as many of my faithfull subjects as were
desirous to follow me or I able to carry with me, that so at least
I might secure them from the utter destruction that threatens them
since that was the only way left me to shew them the regard I had for
& sense I had of their unparaleled loyalty.
Among the manifold mortifications I have had in this unfortunat
expedition, that of being forced to burn severall villages &c as the
only expedient left me for the publick security, was not the smallest
It was indeed forced upon me by the violence with which my
rebellious subjects acted against me, & what they, as the first auth
of it, must be answerable for, not I; however I cannot think of
leaving this Country without making some provision to repair
that loss. I have therefore consign'd to the Magistrats of
the sum of desiring & requiring y
if not as an obedient subject, at least as a lover of your Coun
to take care that it be employ'd to the design'd use, that I may at l
have the satisfaction of having been the destruction & ruin of no
at a time I came to free all. Whether you have yet receiv'd
letter or what effect it hath had upon you I am as yet ignorant
but what will now become of these unhappy Nations is but too pla

Letter written by James Edward Stuart after retreat from Perth (Drambuie Collection).

CHAPTER 13

The Sentence

The morning of February 9th dawned as icy cold as the days that had gone before. The River Thames had frozen hard and an ice fair was being held on its surface. Winifred, though still feeling weak after her illness, was determined to be present at Westminster Hall for her husband's trial. Lord Cowper, the High Steward, had been chosen to preside as judge and to pronounce sentence on the Jacobite lords.

The Whig government had convinced George that it was important to make a great spectacle of the occasion. The hall had been hastily cleaned and cleared of the small stalls and crowds which generally filled it, and the footmen and gentlemen ushers on duty had each been given a new set of scarlet livery.

The tiers of seats which had been built up on scaffolding for the public were filled to capacity and the audience waited expectantly as for a good piece of theatre. The Lords came through from the Upper House and the Members came from the Commons and took their seats on either side of the woolsack. To mark the gravity of the occasion, the Prince of Wales was present in a specially prepared box.

Five coaches, newly painted, brought the High Steward and his officers to the court. Lord Cowper, known to be a stern judge, was an imposing figure in his crimson clothes as he was processed into the hall by the Garter of Arms carrying his wand, followed by the Usher of the Black Rod.

The Jacobite lords, with the exception only of Lord Wintoun who had successfully convinced the lawyers that he was insane, had been brought from the Tower and stood together by the Bar. First the articles of impeachment were read out and then the answers that they had previously handed in were read. They had all been advised by their lawyers to plead guilty but both the Earl of Widdrington and Lord Nithsdale had hoped to extenuate their guilt by expressing the hope that their prosecution would be taken out of the ordinary course of justice.

The High Steward then addressed the assembled prisoners. "My Lords that are prisoners at the Bar, I am to acquaint your Lordships that upon any occasion which shall be offered you to speak for yourselves, you are to direct your speech to the Lords in general and so is any other person that shall have occasion to speak in this court." After calling out the names of the prisoners he continued: "You stand impeached of High Treason by the Commons of Great Britain in Parliament assembled which treason is contained in the articles that have been lately read; to this you have severally pleaded guilty and are thereby convicted." He then addressed each of the prisoners by name and they were allowed to plead their case.

The hall being so vast an arena, it was difficult for the prisoners to make themselves heard and when it came to his turn Lord Nithsdale's voice was almost inaudible. In answer to the question, "What say you, William Earl of Nithsdale, why judgement should not pass upon you according to the law", he answered with the following speech. "My Lords, I have confessed myself guilty, relying on his Majesty's mercy; and I beg leave to assure your Lordships I was never privy to any plot or design against his Majesty's person or Government, and was unprovided with necessaries for such a purpose; but rashly and inconsiderably with only four of my servants, joined those who appeared in army in my neighbourhood, and was one of the last who went unto them. At Preston, my Lords, his Majesty's general gave great hopes and encouragement to believe that surrendering to his Majesty's mercy was the ready way to obtain it, with repeated assurances I submitted myself, and still entirely depend on his Majesty's goodness, earnestly beseeching your Lordships and the Honourable House of Commons to intercede with his Majesty on my behalf. And I solemnly promise your Lordships I shall, during the remainder of my life, pay the utmost duty and gratitude to his most gracious Majesty, and the highest veneration and respect to your Lordships and the Honourable House of Commons."

The Lord High Steward then asked each prisoner in turn whether he had pleaded anything in arrest of judgement. Each answered in the negative. For a moment a deadly silence fell on the auditorium, and then Lord Cowper began his address to the prisoners.

"James, Earl of Derwentwater, William, Lord Widdrington, William, Earl of Nithsdale, Robert, Earl of Carnwarth, William, Viscount Kenmuir, William Lord Nairn, you stand impeached by the Commons of Great Britain in Parliament assembled of High Treason in traitorously imagining and compassing the death of his Most Sacred Majesty, and in conspiring for that end to levy blood and destructive war against His Majesty, in order to depose and murder him, and in levying war accordingly and proclaiming a Pretender to his crown to be king of these realms; which impeachment is as much a course of proceeding, according to the common law, as any other whatsoever. If you had been indicted, the indictment must have been removed and brought before the House of Lords (the Parliament sitting). In that case, you had it is true, been accused only by the grand jury of one county; in the present the whole body of the Commons of Great Britain are by their representative your accusers."

He then discussed the pleas they had offered in mitigation of their offences. These, he argued, could not be admitted as an extenuation of their guilt. He made one exception which was the temptation which the Earl of Nithsdale, and others who professed the religion of the Church of Rome, had to engage in this treason, namely, that success on their part must for ever have established in this kingdom the religion which they professed.

He had now come to the climax of the proceedings, paused and drawing breath, started to pronounce the sentence. "And now my Lords, nothing remains but that I pronounce upon you (and sorry I am that it falls to my lot to do it) that terrible sentence of the law which must be the same that is usually given to the meanest offender in the like kind. The most ignominious and painful parts of it are usually remitted by the grace of the Crown to persons of your quality; you James Earl of Derwentwater, William Lord Widdrington, William Earl of Nithsdale, Robert Earl of Carnwarth, William Viscount Kenmuir and William Lord Nairn return from whence you come. There you must be hanged by the neck, but not till you be dead for you must be cut down alive; then your bowels must be taken out and burnt before your faces, then your heads must be severed from your bodies divided each into four quarters; and these must be at the king's disposal. And God Almighty be merciful to your souls."

Having delivered this terrible sentence, the Lord High Steward took his place among the officers of the court and gradually processed out of the Hall. The prisoners were taken back to the Tower to await the announcement of the date of their execution. Three days later, on the Saturday, the warrant for their execution was signed, the execution being appointed to take place the following Friday. As was the custom, even capital punishment was according to the prisoner's rank. For lords of the realm the method of execution would be decapitation by the sword.

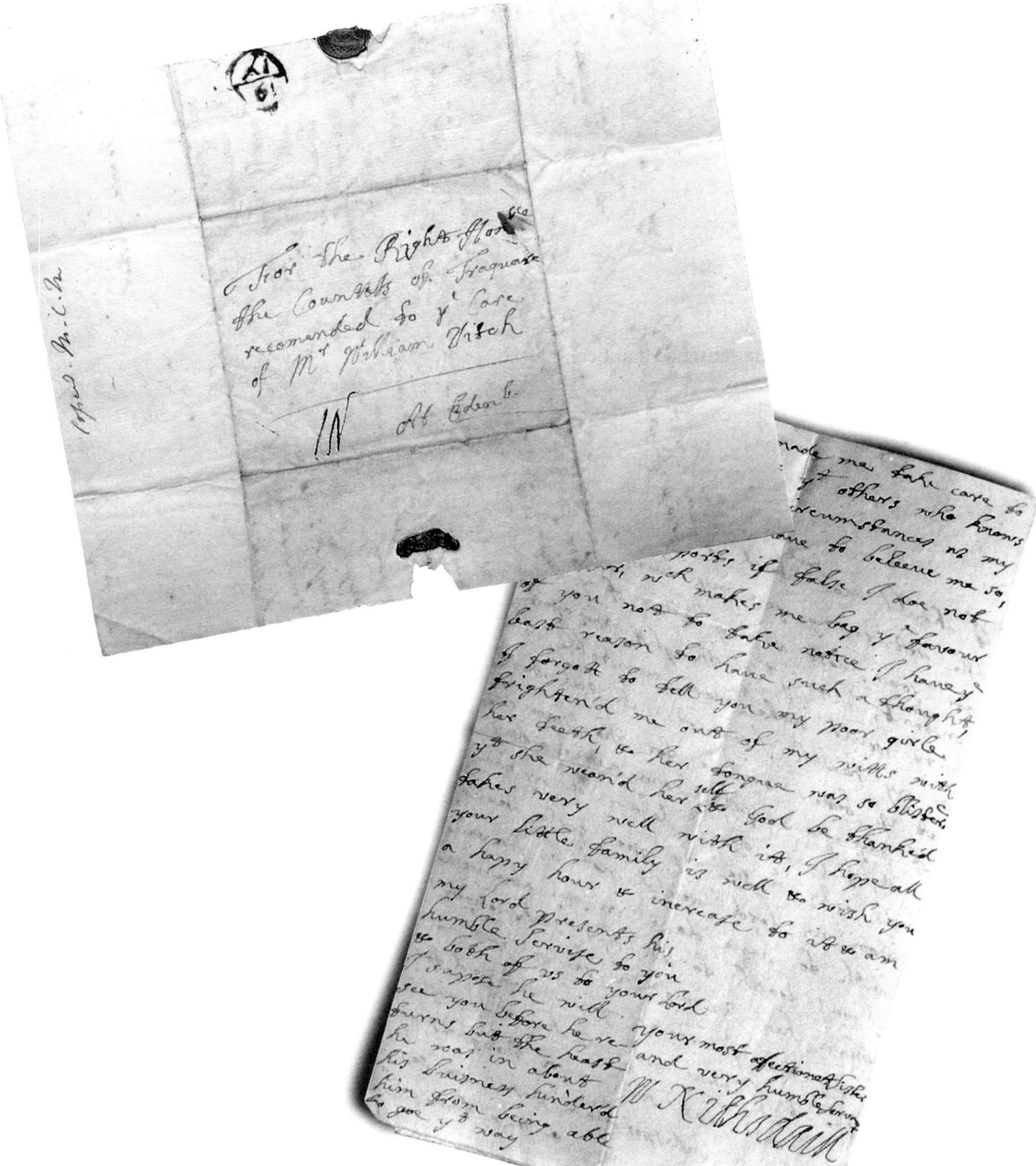

For the Right Honble
the Countess of Traquair
recomended to ye Care
of Mr William Vitch
W At Edenb.

...made me take care to
...yt others who knows
...circumstances as my
...one to beleeue me so,
...ports if false I doe not
...t, wch makes me beg ye favour
of you not to take notice I haue ye
least reason to haue such a thought
I forgott to tell you my poor girle
frighten'd me out of my witts with
her teeth, & her tongue was so blisterd
yt she wean'd her self
takes very well with it, God be thanked
your little family is well & wish you
a happy hour & increase to it & am
my Lord presents his
humble Servise to you
& both of us to your Lord
I suppose he will
see you before he re-
turns but the feast
he was in about
his buisness hinder'd
him from being able
to goe yt way
your most affectionat Sister
and very humble servant
W Nithsdaill

CHAPTER 14

Interceding with George I

Once the sentence had been passed, Winifred and the relatives of those who had been condemned to death lost no time in soliciting anyone who they thought could help them to obtain a reprieve. The cruel treatment suffered by the rest of the prisoners taken at Preston had disgusted the public and it was hoped that this might work in their favour. At least twenty-six of the minor leaders had been executed in Lancashire by order of the High Sheriff. The rest, many of whom had only been drawn into the Rebellion as servants to their masters, were at first crammed into churches in Preston where they were left frozen and starving, and then, "like beasts in the field", herded into overcrowded prisons where pestilence was rife and where many of them died. Finally, they were compelled to cast lots so that only one in twenty was drawn to stand trial. Once condemned, they were all sold as forced labourers to work on the plantations in the West Indies at a price of forty shillings a head.

As he had expected, William Nithsdale was kept closely guarded. He had not been allowed to bring his own servant in with him and the authorities refused to let Winifred visit her husband unless she stayed with him permanently. This she refused to do on the grounds that her health was poor, knowing that it would prevent her from pleading his case. Being only too well acquainted with the way the Tower was run, she knew she would be able to obtain visits by the simple method of bribing the guards.

The prisoners had to provide themselves with all their own food, candles and needs and, unless they had visitors from outside, they were entirely dependent on the servants attached to the Tower. These gentlemen were notorious for cheating the prisoners.

As always, even at this dire moment in their lives, the Nithsdales were chronically short of funds. Winifred had only been able to borrow £100 from Commissioner Alves as a personal favour and the costs were mounting. She was determined not to beg from the Traquairs and had been upset to hear that William had already drawn £100 on Lord Traquair's credit. She wrote to them at once to apologise.

King George hoped to gain popularity by announcing that all the money from the rebels' estates would be put towards paying off the heavy cost of putting down the Rebellion and William had been notified that Terregles had been sequestered and now belonged to the government.

Financial ruin was a real threat to prisoners; to such an extent that a Mrs Collingwood who wrote to a friend in London asking if she could plead for her husband's life only received a reply asking her whether she was mad. If her husband died, her friend pointed out, she would receive her jointure, while if he lived they would not have a groat. She told her to think about it and that she would do nothing until she had received her reply. By the time it arrived the unfortunate man was dead.

Fortunately, William too had a wife desperate to save him against all odds and having great faith in his wife's charm and powers of persuasion, he felt sure that if she were to present a personal petition to the king he would not be able to refuse her. Winifred herself was less confident and had already, together with some of the other wives and well-wishers, set about having a general petition presented to Parliament. However while this was being prepared, she agreed to go to court in person. She was becoming more and more afraid that, even if some reprieves were granted, William would not be one of the lucky ones, since his presence as a Catholic and Jacobite in the south west of Scotland had been a thorn in the flesh of the government for many years. It was still remembered that his grandfather had defended Caerlaverock for Charles I until it had been the last stronghold in Scotland and she was sure that "now they had him [William] in their power they were resolved not to let him slip out of their hands".

However, she was desperate enough to grasp at any straw, and she had a private petition drawn up at once. On the Monday evening, assisted by the sympathetic Evans, she dressed herself in a black manteau and petticoat, as if she were in mourning, and persuaded Mrs Mills to accompany her to St James's Palace where a Drawing Room was being held. Mrs Mills, in turn, had recruited her friend Mrs Morgan, who attended the court frequently and would be able to recognise the new king and point him out to her.

It was the established custom in England that every one of the king's subjects had the right to present him with a petition. George, fearing that some of the unfortunate wives of the condemned lords might approach him, had let it be known that he wished them to be kept away but he could not refuse admittance to that evening's reception to those who were normally accepted at court.

The ladies were admitted to the palace with the rest of London society and, when they heard that the King had not yet left his closet, went to sit in the low panelled room which they knew he must pass through. Here, there were three low windows along the wall, each with a seat, and the women took their places in the central one, passing the time watching the courtiers and ladies and gentlemen gossiping and walking to and fro.

Presently a door opened and the thick-set figure of the king emerged from his closet at the far end of the room and, chatting lesiurely to his gentlemen in German, strolled past them.

Prompted by a nudge from Mrs Morgan, Winifred left her seat. Falling on her knees in front of the king, she held out her petition to him, saying in French (the only language they had in common) that she was the unhappy Countess of Nithsdale, but he refused to pay any attention to her and continued to walk straight ahead as if she were invisible. Frantic that he might pass on without taking the paper, Winifred caught hold of the hem of his coat and attempted to thrust the rolled paper into his pocket. Still he did not stop, but she clung on so tightly that she was dragged along the floor until one of the gentlemen put his hands around her waist to restrain her and another released the king's coat from her hand.

The petition dropped to the floor and was at once picked up by one of the courtiers and delivered to the Lord of the Bed Chamber who, that evening, happened to be Lord Dorset, a friend of Mrs Morgan. Knowing that Lord Dorset was to be on duty that evening, Mrs Morgan had already written him a letter asking if he would be kind enough to see that the petition was read out. This letter she now passed to him as he played cards with the Prince of Wales in the Drawing Room.

As the ladies were about to leave, the Duke of Montrose, an acquaintance of Winifred's, saw them and was about to come over but Winifred signalled him to stay away. She did not want it known that they were friends, so that any support he might give to her petition should be thought impartial.

The next day Winifred heard that, after they had left, her petition had been read by the Prince of Wales. He had considered it kindly and had passed it round and all those who read it had shown a sympathetic interest. She also heard that the courtiers who had witnessed the king's rudeness towards her had been horrified and had lost no time in spreading the tale. All were outraged at the new king's boorish behaviour. It had always been said that the King of England never refused a petition, even from the poorest woman's hand, and to treat a lady of her quality in such a manner was thought to be unpardonable. George never forgave her for this damage to his reputation and later on, when all the exiled wives were allowed to receive their jointures, Winifred was the only one excepted.

The general petition was only presented to the House of Lords the day before the execution was due to take place. The Duke of Richmond (the illegitimate son of Charles II and Nell Gwynn) had promised to present it on the previous day but, on the Prince's advice, had failed to do so. However, he had promised faithfully to carry out his promise the next day. In case he should fail them again, Winifred had asked the Duke of Montrose if he would be ready to take on the task and he had agreed to do so.

Before they went in to listen to the debate, Winifred and some of the wives and relations of the prisoners, accompanied by many of the ladies of quality in town, went to the entrance of Parliament House and interceded with the Lords as they went in. They were treated courteously but there were very few who dared to show great friendliness.

Lord Pembroke had asked Winifred not to approach him in public but had sent her a letter promising to speak in their favour, and his speech in the debate gave them most hope. He argued that the king did not have the power to pardon prisoners accused by Parliament and a motion was passed that Parliament should present an address to His Majesty humbly desiring him to grant a reprieve. To the delight of the prisoners' relations, this was agreed. But another lord got up and asked that a clause should be added that the reprieve should not be general but "for such of them that deserved it".

When Winifred heard this her heart fell. She felt sure that it meant that mercy would only be granted to those who turned king's evidence. The motion was carried and was to be presented to the king that evening. Winifred did not stay to listen to the rest of the debate. When, later that evening, she heard that the king's answer had been "that on this and other occasions he would do what he thought most consistent with the dignity of this crown and the safety of the people", she felt certain that she must take matters into her own hands. She had devised a plan to secure her husband's release and now she knew she must put it into action.

CHAPTER 15

The Escape

Time was running short and some preparatory work was necessary if Winifred's plan were to succeed. As soon as she left the House of Lords Winifred ordered a chair to take her straight to the Tower and, when the guards stopped her at each entrance, she pretended to smile at them cheerfully, saying that she had good news for the prisoners as the petition had been passed in her favour. She repeated the same words to the guards at the entrance to the Lieutenant's Lodgings.

She then made her way up the two flights of stairs to the Council Chamber, the large panelled ante-room where the warders assembled outside her husband's cell. Telling the same story to the warders, she pressed a few coins into their hands and told them the news was good and they must drink to the king and the prisoners' health, being careful not to give them too large a sum in case they suspected that they were being bribed. The warders agreed and told the guard, armed with halberd, who stood outside his cell, to open the door.

Once out of their hearing she told William what had really happened and expressed her doubts about the likelihood of a reprieve being granted. She also told him confidently not to worry, for she had thought of another way to save him as long as he trusted her and he did whatever she told him.

William listened to her patiently but during his imprisonment he had resigned himself to death and, helped by the regular visits of Mr Scott, a priest, was prepared for it. Once he was alone he began to write a last letter to Charles and Mary Traquair beginning "My dearest brother and sister". In it he thanked them for all their favours and generosity and then recommended to them his "dearest wife and children, as what is most dear to me after my own soul". He went on to sing the praises of his "dearest wife" of whom "there cannot be enough said to her praise. Everybody admires her, everybody applaudes her, and extolles her for the proofs she has given me of her love". It was then time to write his last speech, the one that he would read from the scaffold before his execution.

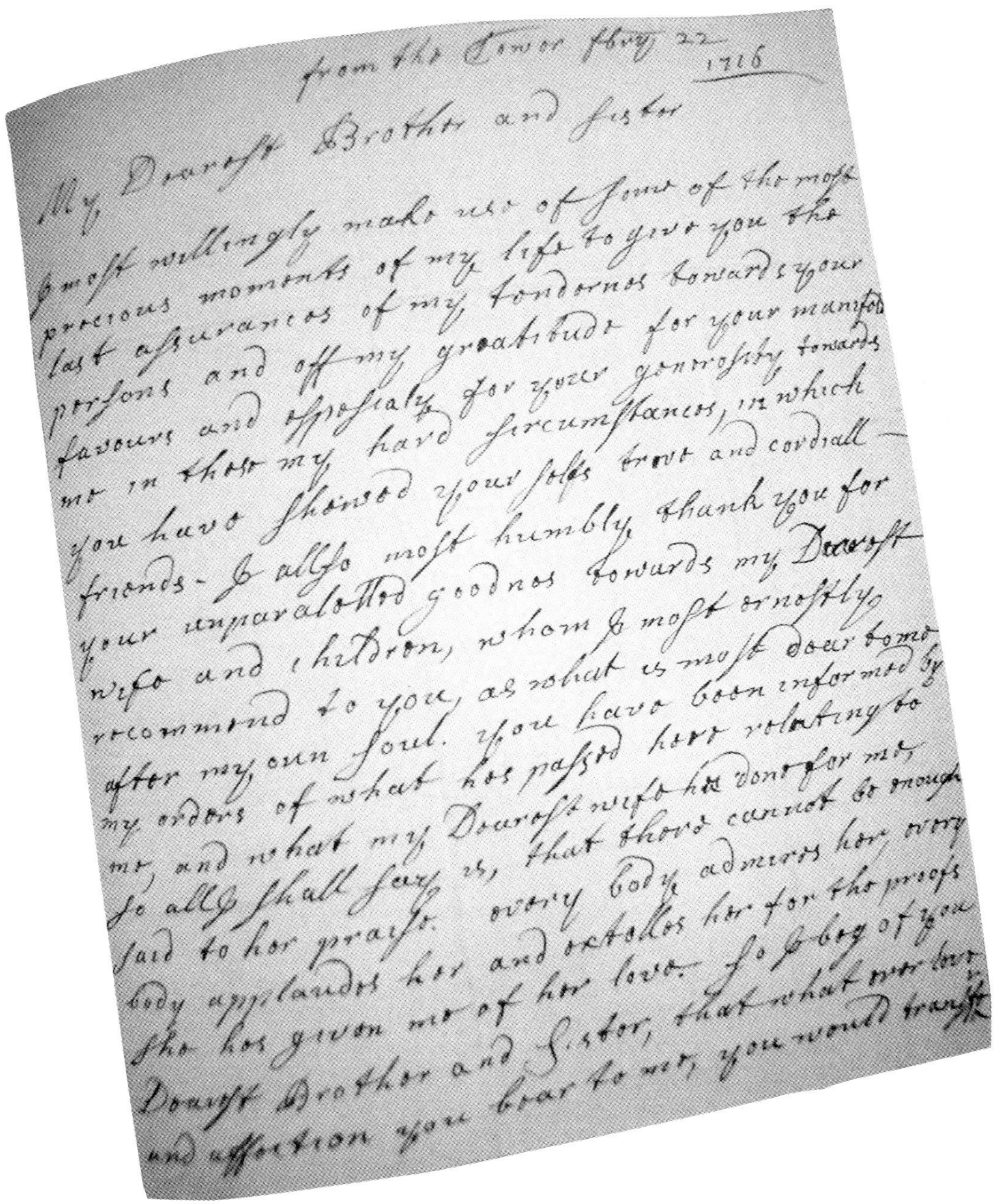

from the Tower ffbry 22
1716

My Dearest Brother and Sister

I most willingly make use of some of the most precious moments of my life to give you the last assurances of my tenderness towards your persons and off my greatitude for your manifold favours and especialy for your generosity towards me in these my hard circumstances, in which you have shewed your selfs true and cordiall friends. I allso most humbly thank you for your unparaleled goodness towards my Dearest wife and children, whom I most earnestly recommend to you, as what is most dear to me after my own soul. you have been informed by my orders of what has passed here relating to me, and what my Dearest wife has done for me, so all I shall say is, that there cannot be enough said to her praise. every body admires her, every body applaudes her and extolles her for the proofs she has given me of her love. So I beg of you Dearest Brother and Sister, that what ever love and affection you bear to me, you would transfe

Lord Nithsdale's farewell letter to the Traquairs from the Tower

"Being in a short time to appear at the tribunal of the sovereign judge of the living and the dead, with whom I have endeavoured to make my peace, and from whom I hope for mercy, I think myself obliged to publish my sentiments to the world. This I owe to God, to my neighbour and to myself. I declare therefore in the first place that I die as by God's grace I have always lived, a true and dutiful son of the Holy Catholic Apostolic Roman Church. Secondly, I declare that I drew my sword merely out of the motives of justice and piety, to assert the undoubted hereditary right of the Prince, whom I then believed, and still believe to be my only liege lord, and lawful sovereign, James the Eighth of Scotland and Third of England, and to deliver my native country from the oppression and misery under which it groans. If I fall victim to so good and glorious a cause, it is what many of my ancestors have done who generally shed their blood for the defence of their king and country. As to any design on the life of him who now possesses the throne (and by whose orders I am now put to death) I take heaven and earth to witness that I never formed or was privy to any such thing. So far was I from such a resolution, that I could not look upon it without detestation and horror. I say the same of any attempt against the ancient constitution of these realms, either in Church or State. Thirdly as to my pleading guilty, I declare that I only intended to acknowledge that I had taken and appeared in arms, for the motives specified; if in my answer to the Articles of Impeachment, or any other writ, I made use of the word crime, I only meant an offence against the present government and not any real crime. However I acknowledge that I am heartily sorry for my weakness for making use of this expression, and crave God's mercy and pardon of those whom I have scandalised or offended by it. Fourthly, and lastly I declare that in imitation of my Lord and saviour Jesus Christ, and in obedience to his most just command, I heartily and sincerely forgive all my enemies, not only those who did or wished me harm, but those also who are most accessory to my death, and thirst most after my blood, earnestly desiring that, by the effusion of the same, the wrath of God justly incensed against these nations may be pacified."

The following day Winifred asked Mr and Mrs Mills to invite Mrs Morgan to come to see her in Duke Street as she had a very important favour to ask of all of them. Eager to do anything possible to help her they foregathered in Mrs Mill's parlour and listened as Winifred unfolded the details of the plan. She expained that she had told the warders that a reprieve was likely, hoping that this would relax their guard, and that she had obtained permission to take in one woman at a time to Willliam's cell to bid him what might still be a last farewell. If they would accompany her to the Tower and remain downstairs she would first take up Mrs Morgan, who would wear an extra petticoat and cloak under her own which, as she was tall and thin, would not show. Once in William's cell she would remove the extra clothes and, after a few words with William, she would leave. Then it would be the turn of Mrs Mills. She would go in sobbing, holding up a handkerchief to hide her face so that she would not be recognised by the guards. In William's room she would immediately take off her cloak and petticoat and put on those left by Mrs Morgan. When Mrs Mills left she would walk out with her face exposed, and in her new clothes, would appear to be a different woman. Finally, William would put on Mrs Mill's clothes. As she was pregnant, his stout form would resemble hers and he would come out holding her handkerchief over his face exactly as she had done, and would look like Mrs Mills when she had gone in. All this time Winifred would appear to be in a state of agitation, for by now the guards would know that the news was bad, and she would pretend to be waiting for her maid to come and accompany her to the Lords to hear a final petition. This would give her the excuse not to linger but to rush her visitors past them in a hurry. Mr Mills' task was to wait below and find a safe house nearby where he could conceal William. Later, when Winifred herself came out, Evans would be waiting to take her to join him.

It was a daring plan, born of Winifred's desperation, and relied heavily on the guards not noticing that two women had gone in and three had come out, but Winifred had arranged it ingeniously so that the one they might question would be Mrs Mills, and, if charged, they would find that she was genuinely a woman visitor.

Winifred had deliberately left telling her co-conspirators to the last minute so that they would have no time for reflection and she now asked them to accompany her to the Tower at once. Charmed by Winifred, they were prepared to do anything to help her, and agreed without hesitating.

Everything had been made ready and Winifred gave the extra cloak and petticoat to Mrs Morgan. The three women then got into a hackney carriage and set off, leaving Mr Mills and Evans to follow later. All the way to the Tower Winifred kept up a lively chatter, terrified that her companions might suddenly realise the possible consequences of the venture and change their minds. Byword Arch was heavily guarded but the guards recognised Winifred and, after checking that she had permission to bring in her friends, waved them on. The hackney carriage proceeded up the hill, turning under the Bloody Tower, where they caught a glimpse of the small barred window of William's cell, high up on the inner wall 40 feet above them, and finally arrived at the Lieutenant's Lodgings.

Once inside the actors knew their parts. Leaving Mrs Mills below, Winifred first took up Mrs Morgan. They climbed the two flights of stairs to the large, panelled Council Chamber, where several of the guards and some of their wives and children were chatting and warming themselves in front of a roaring fire. Remembering the money she had given them the day before, the guards greeted Winifred warmly. Her husband's room opened off this chamber and the guard with halberd stood outside. The head warder instructed him to unlock the door and to allow them to go in.

While Mrs Morgan took off her extra clothing, Winifred begged her husband to do as she told him and all would be well. Before he could protest she was leading Mrs Morgan out of the room, pretending to ask her in a loud, excited voice, as they passed the guards, to please go and find her maid quickly as she must present one final petition that evening.

A sobbing Mrs Mills, her face buried in a handkerchief, was the next to bid William a last farewell and she mounted the stairs to his cell, Winifred's comforting arm around her shoulder. The guards exchanged sympathetic glances and admitted them without a word.

Mrs Mills immediately took off her cloak and petticoat and started to dress in the clothes left by Mrs Morgan, while Winifred began to brush white paint onto her husband's black eyebrows. Telling William to put on Mrs Mills' cloak and petticoat, Winifred led Mrs Mills out. She hurried her past the guards, holding her hand tightly and saying in a distraught voice, "dear Mrs Catherine I must beg of you to go in all haste to find my woman for she certainly does not know what o'clock it is, and has forgotten the petition I am to give, which, should I miss is irreparable, having this one night. Let her make all the haste she can possible, for I shall be on thorns till she comes."

After the departure of "Mrs Catherine", Winifred returned to William's room, where he was awkwardly attempting to put on the woman's clothes. Realising that Winifred's plan was by now half way to completion, he followed her directions without protest and allowed her to rub some rouge on his cheeks. As it was getting dark, and fearing that at any time the servant would come in with the candles, she hurriedly pulled the grey hood of the cloak well down over his head and told him to be careful to keep Mrs Mills' handkerchief over his face. Holding him firmly by the arm she walked between his portly figure and the guards, pretending still to be in a state of great agitation, saying: "Dear Mrs Betty my maid is ruining me by not coming. Please run and bring her here, you know my lodgings. If ever you make haste in your life please do it now for I am almost distracted by this disappointment."

The guards were waiting downstairs but hearing her distress, they quickly opened the door and let William out. Beyond the door she could see Evans waiting with Mr Mills.

Winifred now had the most nerve-racking part of her plan to accomplish. She retraced her steps upstairs, still assuming an air of distraction, and asked to be readmitted to her Lord's room. Once inside, she began to converse as if William were still there, imitating his low voice and moving around the room nervously. When she felt that sufficient time had elapsed for him to have been taken to a safe place she bade him goodnight, saying loudly, with the door ajar, that something serious must have happened to have held up her maid and that there was nothing for it but for her to go on her own. She added that if the Tower was still open, she would come again later that evening, but if not, she would be there first thing in the morning when she hoped she would bring him good news.

As she shut the door she carefully pulled the little string that lifted the latch through to the other side so that it could only be opened from inside the cell. She told the *valet de chambre* who was preparing the candles that her lord was saying his prayers and did not wish to be disturbed until he called. Bidding the guards goodnight and murmuring about the petition in a frenzied manner, she hurried down the stairs, got into one of the hackney coaches that was waiting for hire, and asked to be taken to Duke Street.

Here she found her friends, now in a state of shock, having realised exactly what they had just done. Mr Mills had been so sure that her plan would fail that he had not even bothered to find a house for William to hide in, and when he had seen the burly, cloaked figure coming towards him, he had stood rooted to the ground, thunderstruck. Luckily, the ever-resourceful Evans was there to quickly lead him to the house of a friend of hers nearby.

There was still some business to attend to. Winifred ordered a chair and asked to be taken to the Duchess of Buccleuch. That good lady had agreed to accompany Winifred to court with a petition, and this time to make sure it was safely delivered. At the duchess's house Winifred paid off her chair for fear of being followed, and asked the servant who answered the door whether she was expected. She was, but since the Duchess had another lady with her Winifred said that she would prefer not to go upstairs as she was not fit to be seen in company, but asked if she might wait downstairs and that the duchess's gentlewoman might come down and see her. Through this woman, Winifred presented her humble service to Her Grace, who had so kindly offered to accompany her to court, but begged to tell her that she need not now trouble her as it had been decided to present a general petition in the name of all six of the condemned lords instead. Winifred added she that she would not forget the duchess's kindness in offering to accompany her and would return again to thank her personally.

Her next call was on the Duchess of Montrose. Like the duke, she had been sympathetic to the Nithsdales' cause, but the duchess had felt that she would be unable to receive Winifred in the distraught state she expected her to be in and had left a

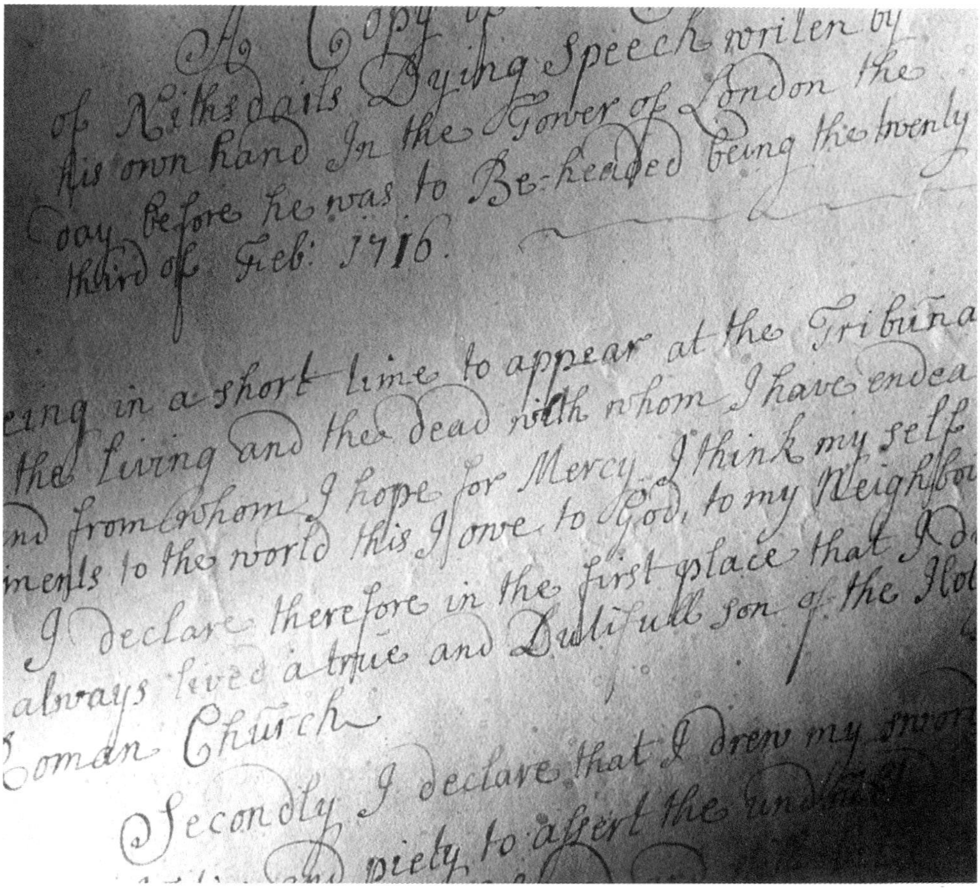

A Copy of
of Nithsdails Dying Speech writen by
his own hand In the Tower of London the
day before he was to Be-headed being the twenty
third of Feb: 1716.

eing in a short time to appear at the Tribuna
the living and the dead with whom I have endea
nd from whom I hope for Mercy I think my self
ments to the world this I owe to God, to my Neighbo
I declare therefore in the first place that I
always lived a true and Dutifull son of the Hol
Roman Church
I declare that I drew my swor
Secondly I declare
piety to assert the

Copy of speech Lord Nithsdale intended to make from the Scaffold.

message with her servant to say that she was not at home. Fortunately her orders had been forgotten, and Winifred was ushered into the drawing room. When the astounded duchess received Winifred, with her clothes dishevelled and her hair untidy but her face glowing with happiness, she thought at first that she had lost her mind. Once she had sat her down and heard the full story, the duchess implored her to go into hiding at once, as she knew the king was particularly ill-disposed towards her. The duchess promised that she would go to court herself that evening to find out how he had reacted to the news of William's excape.

At last Winifred was able to go to the house that Mr Mills had eventually found for William, which happened to be just by the court of guards. It belonged to a poor woman who had a small room upstairs, with one narrow bed in it. Both William and Winifred were obliged to get straight into it in case they made any sound which could be heard below. A bottle of wine and some bread had been left for them, and there they stayed from Thursday evening until Saturday morning.

Council Chamber in the Lieutenant's Lodgings.

CHAPTER 16

William flees to France

And fare thee well, my bonnie gray steed,
That carried me ay sae free,
I wish I had been asleep in my bed,
The last time I mounted thee:
The warning bell now bids me cease,
My trouble's nearly o'er;
Yon sun now rising from the sea
Shall rise on me no more.
LORD DERWENTWATER'S GOOD NIGHT.

When the news of Lord Nithsdale's escape first reached King George it was reported that he stormed with rage and maintained that "such an event could not have happened without connivance". Captain d'Oyley, the Lieutenant of the Tower, was immediately sent for and ordered to give an explanation. Although he managed to keep his own job, five other warders, with ninety years service between them, were immediately dismissed from their posts.

When his anger died down, the king was heard to admit that, "for a man in my Lord's situation, it was the very best thing he could have done". But his resentment of Winifred never abated. Not only had his pride been hurt but his reputation had suffered from the way he had treated her at court and he maintained that she had "done him more harm than any woman in Christendom".

That same evening the remaining five Jacobites were still living in the hope of being granted a last-minute reprieve. Lord Kenmure sent a note to a friend begging him to acquaint him with the news of one as soon as it was known "that I may meet that fate with readiness which in a state of uncertainty I expect with uneasiness". However, when a reprieve did come in the early hours of the following morning, it was for Lords Widdrington, Nairn and Carnwarth. Only Lord Kenmure and Lord Derwentwater were to be taken to the scaffold. There seems little doubt that Lord Nithsdale would have accompanied them. Although his name was written into the reprieve it appeared to have been added later, and it seems that when the authorities discovered that Lord

Nithsdale had escaped his name was quickly included. The question still remains: would he in fact have been granted a reprieve if his wife had not rescued him? It adds an intriguing dimension to the story and may have well given the Nithsdales something to ponder over during their long years in exile.

Lord Derwentwater's relationship to James was the most likely reason that he, in particular, met his fate. The unfortunate young man had been so certain of a reprieve that he had not prepared a speech to read from the scaffold and was obliged to do so hastily that morning. Before he was beheaded he spoke bravely, maintaining to the end, "I am sensible in this that I have made bold with my loyalty having never any other but King James III for my rightful and lawful sovereign". His young wife Ann, who was expecting their second child, was informed of his execution only after it had taken place.

Lord Kenmure died for having been the Jacobite leader in the south west of Scotland. He had not even prepared himself with a suit of black clothes and went to the scaffold dressed in brown. He declined to make a dying speech and wrote to a friend that if one was circulated after his death, as was the custom, he relied on him to declare it to be false. In this last letter he emphasised his adherence to the Protestant religion "practised in the Church of England governed by bishops and that I abhor all king killing doctrines that are taught by the Church of Rome as dangerous and absurd and though I have joined with some that have taken arms of that persuasion, no other notice but that of exercising my loyalty to the person called Pretender, whom I firmly believe to be the true son of the late James II."

The two lords were led out in turn to the scaffold which had been erected on Tower Hill the day before. It consisted of a small platform, draped in black and raised five feet off the ground to afford the excited spectators a good view. Each prisoner mounted the steps where the block stood, surrounded by sawdust, and where the executioner was waiting for them.

Lord Derwentwater's corpse was immediately collected by friends and borne back to his home in Northumberland in an open coffin. That night the aurora borealis was seen and extraordinary coloured curtains of light flashed across the night sky, illuminating his body in strange colours. At his home, the water in the moat was seen to be blood red. All over Britain Jacobites knew that God was showing his displeasure, while the Hanoverians reckoned that it was a sign that justice had been done.

The next day Mr Mills came in the darkness to the Nithsdales' room, bearing bread and wine, and told them what had taken place, informing them also that a price had been put on Lord Nithsdale's head and that it was imperative that he get out of the country as soon as possible. This William agreed to and begged his wife to accompany him. But Winifred was adamant that she should first return to Scotland to collect her daughter

Execution of Lords Derwentwater and Kenmure on Tower Hill (National Galleries of Scotland).

Anne, retrieve the family papers and see what she could salvage from Terregles before the soldiers arrived to take it over, promising faithfully to join him later. There was little time for argument. Mr Mills had contacted a servant, Michele Vezzosi, who worked in the Venetian Embassy and who was willing to help William get across the Channel. His master may well have turned a blind eye to his servant's activities.

William was at first hidden in one of the servant's rooms in the Embassy, but a few days later, when a coach was dispatched to Dover to meet the Ambassador's brother, one of the footmen travelling on the coach in a smart Venetian livery was none other than the 5th Earl of Nithsdale. On their arrival at Dover, Vezzosi negotiated with the captain of a small vessel to take William across the Channel. By the time it was ready to set sail William, who did not suffer hardship easily, had persuaded Velozzi to enter his service, promising that he would arrange for Winifred to bring over his wife and children when she came later. Michele Vezzosi later went into James's service and did not return to Britain again until 1745, when he came as a supporter of Prince Charles Edward Stuart.

The boat set sail for France with the wind behind it and travelled at such speed that the captain made the chance remark that they could not have had a fairer wind if they had been flying for their lives. Once they had landed in France, William and Vezzosi made their way to the Scots College in Paris where Charles Linton and John Stuart gave their uncle a hero's welcome and where a room was quickly made ready for him.

Shortly after his arrival William was overcome by illness and it was several days before he recovered, but as soon as he could he called on Queen Mary Beatrice at St Germain to ask for her help. If St Germain had been thought gloomy in previous years, it was now a pitiable place. Only a few of the old courtiers remained, since all the young and able had accompanied James to Lorraine when he had been ordered out of France.

Mary Beatrice was suffering from cancer and still mourning the death of her daughter, Louise Marie. She missed her old admirer King Louis who had to the end made her feel welcome in France. The new relationship with the Regent, the Duc d'Orleans was very different. Added to this, her financial affairs were worse than ever, since the French pension was required to support not only her own little court but also that of James and, in spite of numerous promises, her jointure had still not been paid. She had sold nearly all her jewellery and was unable to go out in her coach since her horses had died and she was unable to replace them.

However, with her usual spirit, Mary Beatrice made light of her troubles. She was as bright and as kind as ever and received William graciously and gave him a small sum of money. Her advice to him was to join James in Avignon, where the Pope was giving temporary hospitality to the exiles. James, with the help of the Earl of Mar, was trying to find a way out of their troubles and she felt William would be looked after.

It was not long before William received a warm letter from James inviting him to Avignon but warning him that he did not know how long they would be allowed to remain there. "As long as I have a loafe of bread in the world," he wrote, "be assured that you will always have a share of it."

William was encouraged and decided to travel south, hoping that he might be given a position in James's entourage.

CHAPTER 17

Winifred goes into Exile

As soon as they heard that William was out of the country, Winifred and Evans moved into new lodgings in Drury Lane and lay in hiding until they got word of his arrival in Paris. The news of his flight was the talk of the town. It was considered to have been one of the most daring escapes ever to have been made from the Tower and he was the only prisoner to have got away the night before his execution. By the time the story reached the Continent the actual details had become confused and most raconteurs insisted that another woman had been left behind to take Lord Nithsdale's place. The type of riding cloak that he had worn for his disguise became known as a "Nithsdale" and this name continued to be used until the garment went out of fashion.

A reward of £2000 had been put on Lord Nithsdale's head and Winifred had been told that "her head would answer for his", but when it was realised that William had fled the country it was assumed that she had accompanied him and the search was called off. Anxious to come out of hiding and start her journey back to Scotland, she wrote to the Duchess of Buccleuch saying that she heard that she was suspected of having been an accomplice in her husband's escape, but although she could understand that people might think this, there was absolutely no proof that she had been implicated. She therefore asked if she could be given leave to go about her business without being apprehended.

The Duchess put her petition forward. It was at first refused but the Solicitor General decided that, as Winifred had kept a low profile and had made no attempt to parade herself to gain public sympathy, it would be cruel to keep up the search for her. If she continued to keep out of the public eye, no attempt would be made to apprehend her but, if her presence in England or Scotland became generally known, she would be taken into custody.

Winifred agreed to these conditions, and, with Evans and a manservant, prepared for her return to Scotland. She bought saddle horses for the journey, planning to follow a cross-country route on out-of-the-way roads, staying at small country inns where she would not be recognised. Having already survived the journey in rigorous winter weather she felt perfectly capable of making it now in spring.

At the end of April, they arrived at Traquair and for the first time for many months Winifred was able to relax in the company of her welcoming relations and be reunited with her beloved daughter Anne. The little girl had settled in happily with her cousins and had become the pet of her aunt, who had taken a particular fancy to the child.

The Lord Lieutenant of the County, a friend of Charles Traquair, had promised to notify them in advance if a search was to be carried out, and Winifred also took the precaution of letting it be known that she had come to Scotland with the leave of the government, so she had nothing to fear. After resting for two days she was anxious to move on to Terregles. She knew that the house, its contents and the estate now officially belonged to the government and was desperate to remove everything possible before the Commissioners came to take it over. She was also extremely anxious to retrieve the buried family papers which proved that the estate had been made over to her son.

On her arrival at Terregles, Winifred sent word to all her neighbours asking them to come and see her and told the servants who came to welcome her that she had been given permission to go back to her old home. The house had been searched many times and it was with some trepidation that she approached the terrace, accompanied by her gardener. To her relief, she found that the hiding place was untouched and that the papers, which must have been hard frozen during the winter, were perfectly dry and in the same condition as when she had first put them there.

The next day, with the help of Evans and Marian Irving, another loyal friend and servant, Winifred began to remove and to sell as much of the household furnishings as she could. Winifred had not lived in exile for nothing and knew how desperate their situation might become. The more that she could sell and take with her, the more grateful they would be for it later on. Together the women stripped the house.

After a few days she was warned that the magistrates in Dumfries were suspicious and were coming over to see her papers. Pretending that she would be only too pleased to see them and saying that she wondered why they had taken so long to come and pay their respects, she secretly made preparations to depart, and take refuge once again at Traquair.

From there she organised the packing-up of the house and made plans for the management of the estate, before it was taken out of her hands. Major Maxwell undertook to carry out her wishes. Most of the furniture was to be sold, "the cabinet in her closet and the tables and stands". There were only a few pieces that she did not wish to part with: "The chairs from the walnut tree dining room, the chairs in the velvet room, the feather bed belonging to my Lady Dowager's bed and the best of the other feather beds. Two of the quilts, the little one from the silk dressing room and the cleanest of the big ones, and the upper part of the silk dressing room bed which must be packed well or it will be quite spoilt." All these items were trundled over by cart to Traquair where her sister-and brother-in-law had agreed to store them. The cows were to be sold, all save the best two which must be brought to Traquair, and the grass in the meadows and three "bols" of malt she had seen in the Brew House. She wanted the park to be let and asked particularly that the stable should be kept locked and the horses well looked after, as she would need them again for her return journey. She had not lost all hope of returning to Terregles one day, for when she heard that some trees had been cut down, she wrote at once to Major Maxwell saying she hoped they were not near the house for this would upset William, adding that if the money was not needed for repairing tenants' houses she would like to have it sent over immediately. Everything had to be done as quickly as possible and she realised sadly that this was not the best way to obtain good prices.

The loads of worn but well-loved items that had made up her home soon began to arrive at Traquair. This was a moving sight for Winifred, whose fifteen years at Terregles had been happy ones, spent in the only home of their own that the she and William were ever to have. Mary Traquair too was stirred by the sight of the familiar objects. The two families began to remember things they did not want to part with. The Traquairs would like the "great bird cage" and the "grey bed if a decent price cannot be got for it". They did not want it sold for a song. Winifred remembered the cold still and "the little copper thing that stood beside it". Although she knew it was a pity to sell the "great copper" as it would be expensive to renew, she had heard that the soldiers were already on their way across the border and it would only be stolen.

By the end of May, Winifred's task was complete. Major Maxwell had surpassed her expectations in the prices he had obtained and Marian Irving and her sister had loyally obeyed her every order in the sad task of dismantling the house. When some of the neighbours told her that "she should not be meddling with rebels goods" the stalwart woman had replied that "Her Ladyship is no rebel and the things are hers".

Winifred's final letter of thanks elicited the following reply: "Dearest Madam, I am really ashamed of the notice your Ladyship is pleased to take of the small service my sister and I has done on this occasion....I pray God send your ladyship a quick and happy meeting for I am sure it would be my Lord's greatest felicity to meet his dear preserver and I assure your Ladyship I am sorry I cannot be a witness to the joyful meeting." She thanked Winifred for the offer of anything she would like to have from the house but "will take no presents as long as we can sell" and ended by saying that Major Maxwell had just repaid her for a debt she was owed but that "if your Ladyship thinks you will want money for your journey I will very joyfully return what I have got".

By now Winifred was certain that she was pregnant. She had also received a letter from William urging her to join him in France and she knew that she must travel down to London soon, before the pregnancy was too far advanced. She decided to go once again by horseback as she found that, in her condition, a horse with an "easy trot" was more comfortable than being bumped along in a coach. This time she was to be accompanied by her daughter Anne and her nurse, Mrs Lindsay, as well as Evans.

It was a sorrowful parting. Winifred knew she was saying goodbye to the family she loved and could rely on above everyone else and they all knew that they might never see each other again.

London had been heavily garrisoned after the Jacobite trials with 3000 foot guard as well as horse dragoons on duty day and night. Earlier in the summer people had been apprehended for wearing white roses in the street and three gentlemen had been killed for showing Jacobite support on James's birthday.

Although George considered that he had shown ample mercy towards the rebels, many of his subjects thought otherwise. Stories circulated about his insensitivity and severity towards the prisoners. On his way to catch the boat for one of his many visits to "my kingdom in Germany" he had passed a group of Jacobite prisoners who had been condemned to death. At the sight of the king their hopes were raised, for there was an old custom that the royal face always carried mercy. They appealed to him in vain. His carriage passed them without a sign of recognition. A young Anglican clergyman, William Paul, recently hung drawn and quartered for his part in the rebellion, had so moved the crowd with his final speech that it was said he had attracted more converts to the Jacobite cause than his horrible death had deterred.

When Winifred reached London she felt unwell. She calculated that she was at least four months into her pregnancy and yet she was not yet "quick". In spite of having received another urgent letter from William to join him at once in France, she decided to first go and stay with Lucy in the convent in Bruges where she could give birth to her baby and be looked after with little expense. While they waited in London to catch a boat to Ostend, Winifred tried to contact her family to see if any of them were able to give her financial help but none were in a position to do so. Her brother William, now the 2nd Marquis of Powis, was the only member of the family to have made his peace with the government and was in the process of getting back the family estates. Winifred had a brief meeting with him and was able to put her family papers into his hands but the only financial help he could offer was to pay her back ten guineas which he owed her.

On a warm July evening the small party consisting of Winifred, who was travelling under the assumed name of Mrs Joanes with her daughter Miss Joanes, Cecilia Evans, who had assumed the name of Powell, Mrs Lindsay and the Vezzosis, embarked on a small vessel at Gravesend, bound for Ostend. They were travelling as ordinary passengers to avoid recognition and shared a cabin with seven others of both sexes.

The boat had scarcely left the harbour when a freak summer storm blew up and the small boat was battered by the waves, plunging and rising so that they all became violently sick. The strength of the waves delayed their progress and Winifred, who had been vomiting for two days and nights, started to miscarry. Mrs Lindsay and Evans did their best to look after her as she lay on a mattress in the crowded cabin and the boat continued to lurch its way towards the Belgian coast. Evans had nursed Winifred through childbirth and miscarriages before but she had never seen her in such distress, and soon began to fear for her mistress's life. Mrs Lindsay agreed that they should tell the captain who they were, and ask if he could allow them to land. With great skill he managed to put in at Sluce not far from Bruges, and Winifred was carried ashore and taken to lodgings, where she was nursed until she was well enough to travel by coach to Bruges and into the care of her favourite sister, Lucy.

English Convent Bruges (English Convent).

It was a moving experience for the two sisters to meet again twenty-four years after their parting at St Germain-en-Laye. Lucy was now Mother Prioress and had already left her mark on the convent by extending the grounds to make a playground for the school and adding a low, vaulted cloister onto the mellow brick building, where the nuns could take exercise, and say their prayers while at the same time benefiting from the fresh air. At one end, near the laundry, the ceiling had been heightened to allow the nuns' white cotton habits to be hung out and blow like great sails in the wind to dry. In an adjoining building the nuns ran a school for girls, mainly from English families who could only get a Catholic education for their daughters on the Continent.

In the peace of the convent, surrounded by the love and kindness of the nuns, Winifred slowly recovered her health.

Altar chosen by Lady Nithsdale for the English convent in Bruges (English Convent).

CHAPTER 18

Searching for a Home

The Papal town of Avignon felt itself honoured to have the Stuart claimant and his followers in their midst and had put several houses at their disposal, but the future was uncertain for the British government was putting pressure on the Pope to move them further afield. The threat of persecuting the Catholics in Britain, though subtly expressed, had to be taken seriously, and the recent loss of prominent Catholics in the rebellion had already weakened the power of those left behind.

While Mar, now James's right-hand man, tried to find a country willing to receive them, Sir William Ellis, the Treasurer at St Germain, brought down 80,000 crowns and tried to work out the best way to stretch the limited means among so many. He advised James to grant as few pensions as possible and to merely pay board and lodging, until it was known who would be staying with him permanently. He also suggested that those, like William, who ate at the king's table, should receive only a "subsistence".

Although hospitality from the local nobility was lavish, William soon became bored at Avignon. He knew that Mar's prejudice against Catholics would prevent him from being given a position at the exiled court. Mar and James, meanwhile, were involved in interminable discussions as to where the court should settle. They wished to remain as near to Britain as possible and were reluctant to cross the Alps to Papal territory in Italy, neither did the Jacobites want to be seen as being under the auspices of the Pope, but it was gradually becoming clear that beggars could not be choosers, and invitations from other countries were notably failing to pour in.

William yearned for his wife and was impatient to see her. Without considering the disfavour he might earn for himself, he left Avignon and travelled to Lille where he found lodgings and begged Winifred to come and join him. Although she was still weak from her illness, Winifred at once left the convent and, with Anne, Evans and Mrs Lindsay, set off for France.

After the initial joy of their reunion the strain of their uncertain future and impoverished circumstances began to tell. Winifred suffered a relapse shortly after her arrival and William blamed her for having made the journey before she had sufficiently recovered.

By the following January it became obvious that they could not continue to live as they were. Even though the kind Queen Mary Beatrice had obtained a pension of 100 livres for Winifred, and had managed to get the Treasurer at St Germain to add an extra 400, it was not sufficient to cover their expenses and she had been obliged to sell a few pieces of the plate that she had brought over with her and which she had hoped to keep in reserve for Anne's education, which she knew was of the utmost importance for only a well-educated and accomplished young lady would be able to find a husband if there was little or no dowry and how else would her daughter survive?

It was an uphill struggle to make William realise the gravity of their position. Winifred knew that he had made a mistake in leaving James and that, if he had stayed, he would eventually have been given a position. When they heard that James had been operated on for a fistula and that he was making a good recovery, Winifred saw a chance to regain the royal favour. She encouraged William to write a letter wishing James a return to good health. He did this in flowery terms ending: "The satisfaction I feel having been once near your person, and consequently witness to those great qualities that must needs render you the darling of your subjects had they the same happiness, makes me more pleased to know that you have made a good recovery."

This note was kindly acknowledged by James and then Mar wrote, telling William that when he was not in the king's service, fifty livres would be docked from his pension. He went on to say that they were soon "to be forced out of Avignon" and it looked as if Italy would be the only alternative. However, he would like William to meet the Emperor's Minister in Brussels and see if they could be found accommodation in Flanders. He had heard the people of Brussels and Flanders are "mighty desirous of having us there". Mar concluded with commiserations for Winifred's illness. "Though I have not had the honour of her acquaintance yet all who have heard of her must honour and esteem her." Mar had confided to others that "a great reward ought to be had to Lady N" but these sentiments were never realised.

When Winifred suggested to her husband that he should return to James while she stayed in France with Anne, he chided her with trying to get rid of him. When she tried to prevent him from always buying "the best of wine and meat" and letting their money run through his fingers, he accused her of denying him the smallest pleasure.

By the spring they were forced to agree on one matter. They must give up their house and move somewhere cheaper. Winifred would have preferred to return to the convent but William was determined that they should go to Paris and that she should visit her old mistress at St Germain and plead for their pensions to be increased. He had also convinced himself that if she went back to England she could make representations to get her jointure returned to her. Several of the Jacobite wives were now claiming their money and had every hope of getting it paid.

As soon as they arrived in Paris, the Nithsdales went to see Father Innes at the Scots College who was busy liaising with Mar to find somewhere for James to settle. The priest was most surprised to see them. As he wrote to Mar: "They of all people will never be suffered to live here, but that Lord's ways are very odd indeed, to speak modestly." "Andrew", (another pseudonym for James), "was mighty mortified at their coming up for no other reason but to go back again and be a new charge."

To Winifred's great relief William was persuaded to go and join James, who had now left with his close followers for Italy, all other offers having fallen through. Winifred was told that it would be unsafe for her to travel to England to try to procure her jointure so she unwillingly made a visit to St Germain, humbly asking the queen if she could help her find a position at either court. The queen received her affectionately but told her gently she could do nothing for her at present. The only encouragement she could possibly give was the gossip that James was looking for a bride. When he got married and had settled his court somewhere he was bound to make more formal appointments. Looking further ahead, when the bride produced a baby, who would be a more suitable governess than Winifred, whose own mother had looked after him.

In the meantime Winifred decided to take lodgings at La Flèche where her son, William Maxwell, was now a boarder in the famous school and where she could live more economically. Before leaving Paris she visited her eldest nephew, Linton, and poured out her troubles. She had been fond of him since he was a child and he was now old enough to be a confidant. She begged him to write to his mother and ask her to write to Lord Nithsdale explaining that if he did not curb his extravagances their life in exile would be a misery. Having already furnished his uncle with several loans when he first came to Paris, Linton understood the predicament and promised to do so.

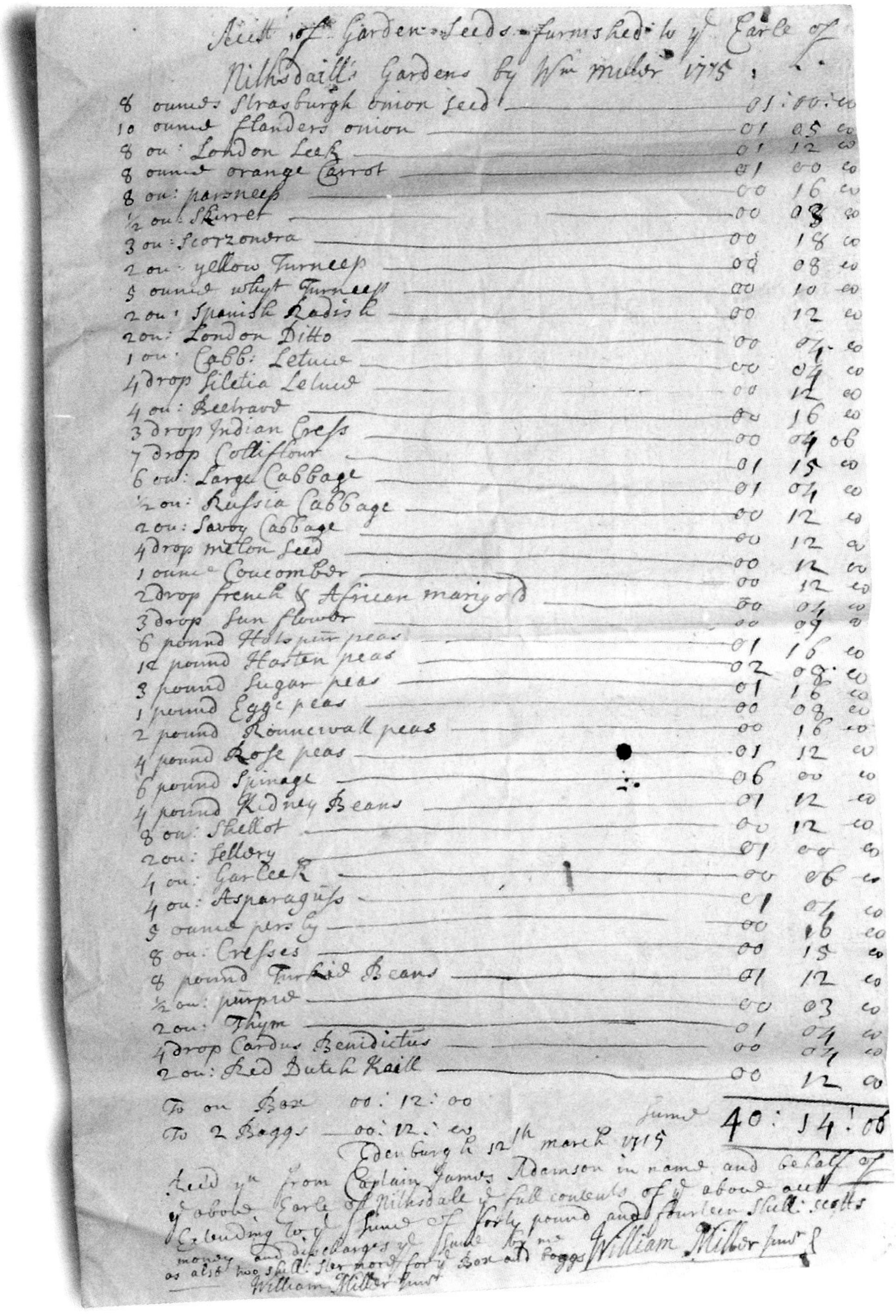

Acctt of Garden Seeds furnished to ye Earle of Nithsdaill's Gardens by Wm Miller 1715 £

8 ounces Strasburgh onion seed	01	00	00
10 ounce Flanders onion	01	05	00
8 ou: London Leek	01	12	00
8 ounce orange Carrot	01	00	00
8 ou: parsneep	00	16	00
½ ou: Skirret	00	08	00
3 ou: Scorzonera	00	18	00
2 ou: yellow Turneep	00	08	00
5 ounce whyt Turneep	00	10	00
2 ou: Spanish Radish	00	12	00
2 ou: London Ditto	00	04	00
1 ou: Cabb: Letuce	00	04	00
4 drop Siletia Letuce	00	12	00
4 ou: Beetrave	00	16	00
3 drop Indian Cress	00	04	06
7 drop Colliflour	01	15	00
6 ou: Large Cabbage	01	04	00
½ ou: Russia Cabbage	00	12	00
2 ou: Savoy Cabbage	00	12	00
4 drop melon seed	00	12	00
1 ounce Concomber	00	12	00
2 drop French & African marigold	00	04	00
3 drop Sun flower	00	09	00
6 pound Hotspur peas	01	16	00
12 pound Hasten peas	02	08	00
3 pound Sugar peas	01	16	00
1 pound Egg peas	00	08	00
2 pound Rouncevall peas	00	16	00
4 pound Rose peas	01	12	00
6 pound Spinage	06	00	00
4 pound Kidney Beans	01	12	00
8 ou: Shellot	00	12	00
2 ou: Sellery	01	00	00
4 ou: Garleek	00	06	00
4 ou: Asparaguss	01	04	00
5 ounce persly	00	16	00
8 ou: Cresses	00	15	00
4 pound Turkie Beans	01	12	00
½ ou: purpre	00	03	00
2 ou: Thym	01	04	00
4 drop Cardus Benedictus	00	04	00
2 ou: Red Dutch Kaill	00	12	00

To on Box 00:12:00
To 2 Baggs 00:12:00
Summe 40:14:06

Edenburgh 12th march 1715

Recd yn from Captain James Adamson in name and behalf of ye above Earle of Nithsdale ye full contents of ye above acct extending to ye Summe of forty pound and fourteen shill: scotts money and discharges ye Same by me William Miller Junr
as also two shill: ster more for ye Box and Baggs William Miller Junr

CHAPTER 19

Urbino

When William set off to meet James in Pesaro he decided to travel to the south of France and from there take a boat to Leghorn. In this way he would avoid the treacherous journey across the Alps in the early spring, when the mountain passes could still be blocked by snow.

The sea proved to be even more hazardous. Such a powerful storm blew up that the sailors gave up all control of the boat and allowed it to be washed up against the coast. They eventually managed to follow the land round to Leghorn where William disembarked, thankful, for the second time in a year, that his life had been saved. Winifred received the news philosophically and wrote back to him saying that she hoped that "two escapes in so short a time is not for nothing and God reserves some great good".

In Pesaro, a small town on the Adriatic coast, Cardinal Davia had put his palace at James's diposal. There William found James, with the Duke of Perth, Lord Panmure and Lord Southesk, in low spirits, having just heard that the British had uncovered their plan to launch a new invasion, this time with Swedish collaboration.

James was also suffering from an affair of the heart. On his way to Pesaro, he had stayed with the Duke of Rinaldo, his mother's uncle, in the beautiful palace at Modena which he had heard his mother talk about so often with longing and nostalgia. There he had fallen madly in love for the first time with the duke's eldest daughter, the beautiful Benedicta who resembled his mother in so many ways. Within a few days he had proposed to her but, although she seemed equally enamoured of him, the duke had not been enthusiastic about the match. He would only say that he would consider the proposal and did not press James to stay longer.

The notable absentee was the Earl of Mar, who had suddenly announced that he had important business to attend to in France and had gone away for a few days but had not returned. It was suspected that he might be sounding out the possibility of returning to the Hanoverian camp.

By May, the temperature began to soar and the Scottish Lords pronounced Pesaro "unwholesome". James needed no prompting to move on to Rome to see what else the Pope had to offer them. Clement X received them formally and invited them to stay at Cardinal Gualterio's residence where James celebrated his twenty-ninth birthday. The Pope ordered St Peter's and the Castel San Angelo to be illuminated in his honour but they were not, however, offered a palace in Rome as a permanent residence and the Pontiff seemed anxious to keep them out of the city.

Instead, the great Renaissance palace built by Frederico da Montefeltro at Urbino in the Umbrian hills was suggested. Frederico had built this pink-stoned "town within a building" out of fees he had earned as a military general. He was a man of great learning and had filled the castle with an extensive collection of books and art; his court had been celebrated as the most cultured in Europe and had become the meeting place for some of the best-known Renaissance artists. However, in the mid seventeenth century the palace had been taken over by the Papal Legate and much of the great collection found its way to the Vatican. Since then the building had become something of a white elephant, and the Pope would be only too pleased to have it occupied. To tempt him further the Pope also offered James a gift of 1200 scudi a year.

The stifling Roman summer soon made the thought of a retreat to the palazzo in the Umbrian mountains inviting and the exiled court duly set off, with James sending out word to all those followers who had not yet found a resting place of their own to come and join him there. At least it would be large enough to accommodate them all.

William was still far from satisfied with James's attitude towards him. Since he was the Catholic of highest rank he had hoped that he might have been given some preferential treatment, at least in the Papal City. But Mar had impressed upon James that his mother had been a bigot and his parents had suffered irreparable damage by being thought to favour those of their own faith. James had made up his mind that this would never be said of him, being well aware that the majority of his supporters, both in exile and in Britain, were not Catholics. Although he never wavered from that religion himself, he had no desire to prevent others from worshipping in any way they wished and wanted this fact to be widely known.

James settled into his private apartments in the castle, leaving the rest of his followers to fit in as best they could. Space was not a problem, but James had brought insufficient servants with him to look after the whole household and was expecting each person to employ his own staff. Even meals were not offered very generously and William soon found his expenses mounting up.

A new cause of irritation was the arrival of an ambitious young man named James Murray. Murray was the same age as James and they had got on well when he had arrived in France as Bolingbroke's secretary. In 1715 he had returned to England and

Great courtyard of Ducal Palace at Urbino.

had been imprisoned briefly. James was delighted to see Murray and he soon took the place of the absent Mar and drove a wedge between the king and his older followers. They felt that he had not sacrificed as much as they had and they resented the fact that this "white livered jackanapes" now appeared to be running the court.

William wrote frequently to Winifred expressing his dissatisfaction, finally announcing that he intended to return to France that autumn for "there is nothing in this damnable country that can tend either to the good of one's soul or body" and that the only satisfaction he could propose to himself was to "be near her person".

Winifred's answer was firm. Though having "her dear Lord with her would be the greatest natural satisfaction she could have in this world," she pointed out that it would be a great mistake for William to leave so soon. It would be said that he had only gone out to Italy to travel at his master's expense or that he only served his master as he could not "live on what he had".

As summer turned to autumn, the king and his court became bored and depressed. The Duke of Rinaldo had finally refused James's offer for the hand of his daughter, afraid of upsetting the British Imperial Alliance. Urbino might have been a magnificent setting for a reigning monarch but for an uncrowned king trying to regain his throne it seemed more like a prison. They were on the brow of a hill too steep to hunt and in an isolated position. As winter drew on it snowed frequently and they were often cut off. The vast palace, with its marble halls, few fireplaces and open courtyard, was cold and draughty and made the Scots lords long even more for their thick-walled, small-windowed castles at home. The fact that the Scots outnumbered the English by ten to one was another cause of friction in this close community.

The sudden return of Mar, with no explanation for his absence, was a welcome distraction. He again took complete control of the household and though one member feared "he would rule England through the king should a restoration ever take place", he was infinitely preferable to Murray, who now took a back seat.

Although Mar was a rogue, like many rogues he was good company. He realised at once that his companions were in need of *divertissement.* He organised games of shuttlecock in the beautiful Renaissance courtyard to give them exercise and ordered painting and drawing materials to be brought into the palace. Musical evenings were arranged and invitations were issued to the local nobility. Many of them had beautiful daughters and mild flirtations passed the time for those unimpressed by the music. Mar also went out of his way to taste the different wines in the region and encouraged his countrymen to develop their palates and drink with more discrimination.

Even Mar, however, could not pretend that their life was interesting. He wrote to a friend: "We are going on in our own dull way, one day being as like another as two eggs and them eaten without pepper or salt."

CHAPTER 20

James seeks a Bride

Here's a health to the mysterious Czar
I hope he'll send us help from afar
To end the work begun by Mar.
JAMES HOGG

La Flèche was a peaceful, small town south west of Paris in the flat, fertile valley of the River Loire. It was dominated by the great buildings of the Jesuit College, founded in 1607 by Henry IV, which had become one of the most famous Catholic schools in France and where Sir George Maxwell had decided that William should complete his education. William had grown into a large young man of seventeen who, except for his physique and fair colouring, had taken after neither of his parents.

Winifred engaged masters for Anne, now a bright little girl of eight. She was instructed in French, singing, dancing and the harpsichord, and Mrs Lindsay made sure that she wrote and read in English each day so that she would not forget her native language. She was also obliged to work at her sampler and had already embroidered twenty-four letters, "twice over and both sides alike". William, who received his lessons at the college, was also being given extra lessons in dancing and the harpsichord.

Winifred received frequent visits from her two nephews, Linton and John. The two brothers were turning into sophisticated young men and Linton had decided that his studies were complete and he was about to set off for Italy on a "tour of improvement". For the benefit of his parents, who were to finance the expedition, he had put forward the various methods of transport he could use and neatly proved why he must choose the most comfortable and also the most expensive: the "common voiture" had the disadvantage that he must rise early and arrive late so there was no time to see anything on the way; going by post or hired horses would expose him to the " injuries of the seasons" and was much opposed by his friends who were "solicitous" about his health, while the Italian chaise, which "all computed will not much increase the expense", was by far the most convenient way to travel. Before leaving he came to see Winfred, as when he arrived in Italy he hoped to pay his respects to his uncle and to the king.

John, who never wished his studies to interfere with his social life, had moved to another school, the College of Plessis. When Winifred, hoping to save his parents money, had suggested the celebrated Acadamy in Angers instead she realised she had quite upset the apple cart. John immediately explained why he could not possibly leave Paris and go there. It was "very dangerous for the bad company that there accrues" and the young Englishmen who went there had "debauched all the pensioners at Angers both to expense and manners". Moreover, he assured her, Paris was no more expensive than Angers.

Winifred and Mary Traquair kept up a regular correspondence. Winifred worried about Terregles which was standing empty and she asked that peats might be cut and fires lit to prevent it from getting damp. In return she sent back friendly reports to Mary on her two sons.

Winifred settled contentedly into her new life and managed to keep her household and pay for Anne's lessons on her pension, but only because each month an extra amount was added to it by the personal direction of the queen. Knowing that this situation could not last for ever, she took the queen's advice and kept her ears open for rumours about James's marriage. She was determined that as soon as this happened she would apply for a position in his household. When she heard it said that he was to marry the Duchess of Courland, a niece of the Czar of Russia who had always had a leaning towards the Stuart cause, she wrote to James at once to congratulate him on his forthcoming marriage, requesting that she might be allowed a place in waiting on his queen. She pulled no punches in listing her credentials, "if my father losing all he had to follow his late Majesty and dying in his service, and my mother in yours, be not sufficient motives to induce me to hope for it. I am married into a family whose ancestors can produce constant losses from father to son for their loyalty, and my present Lord after having lost the remainder on the same account, and being within a few hours of losing his head also on a scaffold for having endeavoured to serve your present Majesty, I can never persuade myself you will refuse me the favour I so earnestly beg."

By the time James received this letter the negotiations for this marriage had come to a sudden halt. It had been discovered that the Duchess's parents had not actually been married when their daughter had been born and this was considered to render her quite unsuitable. James replied to Winifred that the "supposition you go on is not yet come to pass". He added that, when it did, he would not be increasing his household and tactfully continued, "as to my wife, whenever I have one, the number of persons of quality and merit now banished on my account and the uncertainty of my abode and all that relates to me, which will continue long as I am abroad, have made me long since abolish fixed waiting and resolve to take no persons into my family as what was most suitable to my circumstances and would be generally most agreeable by avoiding all apparent preference and partiality." He told her that he had already refused many persons of distinction, otherwise, "your husband's merit had not been forgot". The letter finished: "After this, if it be convenient for Lord Nithsdale's and your circumstances to live where my future wife and I may happen to be, you may be sure to be very welcome, and this I shall endeavour to make your husband's whose singular merit with me I can never forget, no more than the particular care the late Duchess of Powis had of me as a child."

When Winifred received this letter she was uncertain how she should act and sent it to Queen Mary Beatrice to ask for her advice. The queen was unwell, and it was several weeks before Winifred received the following letter, one of the last letters the queen was to write. "I am so guilty toward you in point of writing that I must begin by asking your pardon for it and assure you that it is not for want of kindness but, I have so much writing to the king that I seldom have time or strength left for other letters, and this I hope you will believe and excuse once and for all. I am sorry the king has not granted your request, however his letter is kind, and the leave he gives you to go and stay wherever he shall settle with his Queen, I think ought not be accepted by you, without you saying that you will expect to be sent for. 'Tis I tell you as a friend and only to yourself, for I would not so much as have you write to your Lord that I say so, but only, that, when the time comes, you will make use with pleasure of the permission I give you. The king had sent me your letter to him and the copy of this to you before you sent it to me, for he knows the kindness I have for you, and how much I wish you about his wife, as soon as he has one, for I write about it to him before you did, and I was glad to tell him that you had not asked it of me, as in truth you had not then, but I am sorry I have succeeded not better, and I desire nobody may know this but yourself unless it be Father Maxwell, to whom I shall explain this matter to shorten my letter and only to tell you that you may count upon my kindness, which I shall always show you when in my power, but this matter does not depend on me, if it did you would have reason to be pleased, as well as with my giving you some succour in the hard circumstances you are in, if I were able to do it, but my own are such, that at present I cannot give the least help to my best friend which is no small grief to me, but, if ever I am in better condition, you shall be too."

At Urbino, renewed efforts were being made to find a suitable bride for James. He was aware, as were his followers, that it was imperative that he should produce an heir, for what would be the point of restoring him to the throne if there was no one to follow on after him? George I might be at loggerheads with his son but he did at least have one, and a grandson too to take his place.

After the negotiations with the Czar's niece had foundered, Mar selected a young Irishman, Charles Wogan, to go in search of further possibilities for a suitable spouse. The first was the Princess Baden Baden, the daughter of the late King Lewis, and the other a Princess Saxe, a cousin to the King of Poland. Wogan was given the following brief: "if any other courts fall in your way through Germany, where there are princesses, it will not be amiss that you endeavour to see them and inform yourself about them, for there are many in that country and in some of them there may be princesses as fine women as any of the two we have been informed of."

So, like the proverbial fairy story, the young missionary set out on his search across Europe to survey the princesses and returned with his report to the prince. He gave a detailed description of their physical and material assets but each was deficient in some respect: "The Princess of Baden is a dwarf", or, "the Princess of Saxony is too old". Finally he came to Clementina Sobieska, the youngest daughter of King James of Poland and granddaughter of the famous King John of Poland, renowned for having saved Christendom from the Turks. With this princess no fault could be found. She was vivacious and pretty, and had enormous charm, and she was also rich and well connected. Her dowry would consist of a large amount of money as well as many jewels and she would also inherit a share of the family estates in Poland, since her father had no sons. Her relations included the Emperor Charles VI himself, and the King of Portugal, the Electors of Treves and Bavaria, and the Prince of Palantine. In addition, Pope Clement, who she was named after, was her godfather and she was a devout Roman Catholic. Wogan reported that, according to his soundings, her father seemed well disposed towards the match and Clementina had confided in him that as a child she used to play at being Queen of England.

Wogan was congratulated on his mission by James, who was still suffering from his rejection by his cousin in Modena and looked on his marriage purely as an act of duty. It was decided that a more important and non-Catholic representative should be sent out to make the final proposal in James's name so as not to upset the Protestant Jacobites in Britain. The ambitious James Murray, always eager to carry out his master's wishes, was chosen for this charge. However, since Clementina would be such an eligible bride, and since she would bring so many new allies to the Stuart side, the House of Hanover would be in real danger from any progeny of the union and it was feared they would do anything in their power to prevent it from taking place. The marriage negotiations were therefore kept as secret as possible.

CHAPTER 21

Winifred goes to Italy

After her long illness, Queen Mary Beatrice died suddenly on 7th May 1718. The queen's last wish was that her son should "persevere in his profession what ever should happen". The members of her small court at St Germain were heart-broken, for not only would each one miss her personally but they did not know what was to become of them, since her small pension had eked out the lives of many of her "family". Winifred also felt bereft. She had "lost a kind mother" she wrote to Mary Traquair, "for she was truly that to me whilst I had her".

Further afield, many who had known her suffered a personal loss. Mr Carnegy, who was looking after the education of the younger Stuart girls in Edinburgh, wrote to Mary Traquair: "She was not only my Queen and best of women but the best friend I had in the world." The French court went into mourning, much to the regret of the English government, who had hoped that sympathy for the Jacobites had died out in France. Oddly enough, in Rome there was some doubt. Linton, who had arrived there, did not hesitate and both he, his companion Mr Panton, and his two servants went into the deepest black.

The death of the queen brought Winifred's respite from pressing worries to an end. Anne fell ill with a fever that was so severe that her life appeared to be in danger. Doctors had to be called in and an assortment of medicines prescribed. Mrs Lindsay and Winifred sat by her bedside until, at last, her temperature subsided. She was severely weakened by her illness and her recovery was very slow. Her lack of appetite required her to be fed on special expensive luxuries and this additional expenditure caused Winifred severe difficulties. As she had feared, when she received her monthly payment from Mr Dicconson at St Germain, the extra 300 livres which had always been added at the queen's request was not included. She wrote at once asking if he could let her have this sum, only to be told that there was no official letter authorising the payment.

Desperate to know how to pay her bills, she wrote to Lord Mar at Urbino telling him of her situation and asking if he could get the king's authorization. Her letter finished with the following paragraph: "I have not yet had the happiness of your personal acquaintance, yet ye great character ye had so justly merited in ye world together with ye obligations I have already had from your Grace on my Lord's account makes me ambitious to owe all to you and if it is not in my power to make any other return, at least I shall be sure to make known to all my Lord's friends and mine how happy we are in your Grace's goodness to us."

Winifred received no answer to this letter, but shortly afterwards one came from William with the news that she must make haste and come to Urbino as soon as possible. James had confided in him that he hoped to be married by the winter and that he wanted them in his "family". If Winifred were on the spot he was sure she would be given a position but it would be "first come, first served as they say; and were you here I am confident my Master would refuse you nothing you could in reason ask for, for he speaks of you with affection and I am sure you would gaine on him every day".

William knew that Winifred could not possibly afford the journey, but the queen had promised Winifred that when she went to join James she would provide the money for the journey. It was a cruel stroke of fate that she had died only a few weeks before it was needed.

William estimated that she would need 3000 livres to cover the expenses and to buy new clothes which would be essential if she were to appear at court. He now proposed that she should write to the Traquairs and ask them to loan this amount against the surety of the furniture which they were storing for them. He was sure that they would understand that this money would be a good investment as, once they had gained a position in James's family, their troubles would be over.

Winifred was loath to be the one to approach the Traquairs - after all, Mary was William's sister and not hers. She felt that the Traquairs had already done enough for them and was aware that the education of their children was already stretching their finances to the limit. A request to her sister, Anne Carrington, was made, but to no avail.

Lady Carrington was still negotiating to get her money sent over from England and she also had been dependent on the pocket of the queen. There was nothing for it but to write to the Traquairs.

Before she received her reply, Mar had started to organise her journey. George Mackenzie, the younger of Delvine, had also been invited to Urbino and it was arranged that they should travel together. A payment of 2000 was made for their joint expenses.

The household at La Flèche was broken up, Anne and Mrs Lindsay travelling to Paris and taking lodgings next door to Lady Carrington who agreed to pay their rent as there was no room for them in her apartment; Winifred was to continue to pay for Anne's education. Evans would accompany Winifred to Urbino.

Shortly before she left, Winifred received an answer from Mary Traquair. For the first time she and her husband were impatient with the frequent requests from the Nithsdales. They found it ridiculous that William should think that a few bits of second-hand furniture could be worth 3000 livres and, far from wanting it, they were at an inconvenience storing it. Why did Lady Carrington feel unable to help they asked? Winifred regetted that she had made the request, especially as now the money was no longer needed.

At the beginning of September, she was ready to leave. Some extra money had been forthcoming from Dicconson, since she was responsible for supporting her companion, Mr Mackenzie, on the journey but she was worried that it would not be enough. She had also been entrusted with the late queen's few remaining jewels which were to be James's wedding present to his bride. Mr Dicconson came to Paris and personally handed them over: three pearl necklaces, diamond earrings and a diamond buckle for a girdle.

Before Winifred left Paris, she received a visit from John Stuart who had been asked by his parents to offer her money should she need it for the journey. His parents, it seemed, had had a change of heart, but Winifred was sufficiently proud not to accept. She had, she said, scraped enough together and would not be a trouble to them. She was however extremely grateful to John when he offered to visit Anne regularly and keep an eye on her and Mrs Lindsay.

Winifred, Evans and their companion Mr Mackenzie embarked on their travels in a chaise which broke down twelve times between Paris and Lyons. From Lyons they proceeded to cross the Alps by Mount Cenis, came down through Turin and travelled from there to Bologna and on up to Urbino. The journey took a little under two months.

James (artist unknown, National Galleries of Scotland)

CHAPTER 22

Removal to Rome

After their arduous journey, Winifred and her companions arrived at Urbino in October. She was given a rapturous welcome by William, from whom she had been parted for over a year. There was a cheerful, relaxed atmosphere about the palace, for the household was in the middle of preparations for a removal to the Muti Palace in Rome which had been offered them as a permanent residence by the Pope, when he had heard of James's engagement. James and several of his courtiers had gone on ahead and everyone was thankful not to be spending another winter among the Umbrian mountains.

The forthcoming marriage was viewed as a triumph. That James might at last be given an heir was exciting enough but that he had captured such an important bride was more than they had dared hope for. Clementina's father was said to be preparing her dowry and among other things she was to bring a large case of family jewels with her. Murray and Wogan had already left to escort her to Bologna where it was planned that she would meet James and the marriage would take place.

There was another cause for optimism. Earlier in the year James had been approached by a new ally. This was the wily Cardinal Alberoni who had achieved his cardinal's hat through James's intercession with the Pope. Alberoni now lived in Spain and had great influence at the Spanish court. By helping James to invade Britain, Alberoni hoped to distract England's attention from the war currently being waged against Spain.

James sent Ormonde, Earl Marischal and his brother James Keith to Madrid, to consult with the cardinal. They decided on mounting two simultaneous rebellions. Ormonde was to command a landing in England, while the Keiths were to organise the Scottish operation. The cardinal had arranged for Spain to support both these enterprises with men, arms and ships. It looked as if a new and more fortunate era might be about to start for James and his homeless subjects.

Shortly after Winifred's arrival at Urbino, Linton appeared at the palace with Mr Panton. Since the previous winter he had been staying in Rome with the Duke of Queensberry, a kinsman and another young gentleman, Lord Johnson. His companions, however, did not share his Jacobite sentiments, and Linton had left them in Rome without telling them where he was going. He had heard of James's forthcoming marriage and was anxious to pay him his respects. In great confidence he was told that Clementina was on her way to Italy and was going straight to Ferrara where it was then hoped the marriage would take place. If Linton started soon he might just arrive there in time. He and Mr Panton were invited to stay for a small party which had been given in honour of Winifred's arrival and where a Signora Inocenza, a great favourite with the gentlemen, sang and played the lute with great charm. Mr Panton, who enjoyed spreading gossip, told them how unpopular "squire Bombler", as Mar was nicknamed, had become in Rome. Mar was trying to bully the Pope into handing over Castel Gandolfo, plus a gift of 40,000 crowns to repair it, and had also been overheard telling Cardinal Gualterio that most of the Scots were living far more comfortably at Urbino that they ever would have done among their "snow and hills at home" and as long as they were given plenty of wine they would all be merry enough.

A few days later William Ellis received orders from James for the final removal to Rome. James was not entirely satisfied with the Muti Palace and was still hoping he might be offered a more important building but they were all to come anyway and, for the time being, fix themselves up as best they could. Everything was to be packed up and James gave orders in meticulous detail. "Fitzgerald must be told to take great care of the two miniature pictures that no wet comes near them". Sir William was ordered to give "10 Spanish pistoles to Don Francesco, the concierge, and five to the Poor Clare nuns and agree with Nairne what small matter should be given to the two or three young clergy who used to serve my mass and if there be any other little present that is fit to be given, he'll take care to do it before he parts." Sir William, he said, was also to take charge of the money and to travel in the Berlin with the saddle horses "which to be sure he will take care should go safely". He was to look for a "proper place at Rome to put the goods in and hire rooms for himself and such servants as need to be lodged".

The rest of the court were to be paid two months salary in advance and find their own way to Rome. No allowance had been made for Winifred as James would not have known of her arrival, but Sir William was determined that he could only allow the Nithsdales fifteen pistoles more without direct orders from James. William wrote off to Mar to remind the king that he now had a wife to provide for. He calculated that his pension for two months would just get the two of them to Rome but after that they would be destitute, and asked for money to be kindly forwarded to them at the Scots College in Rome, for that is where they intended to stay on their arrival.

Just before they set out on their journey to Rome, the news was broken that Clementina had been taken prisoner by the Emperor on her way to Italy and was under arrest in Innsbruck. Fearing that this might happen she and her mother had travelled incognito and every precaution had been taken to keep their journey secret. It had been given out that she was making a pilgrimage to the Holy Shrine at Loreto, but the spies had not been fooled and the real purpose of the journey had soon been discovered. George had put pressure on the Emperor, who regretfully placed her under guard at Schloss Ambras.

Nevertheless, plans for the removal continued as before and James returned to Rome to try to organise his court. The Pope had made it clear that it was to be the Palazzo Muti or nothing but he also offered them a summer retreat, the Savelli Palace at Albano. The Muti Palace was an insignificant building of moderate size and considered by James's subjects to be unworthy of him although the Pontiff had, to sugar the pill, mounted a Papal guard outside, an honour shared only by the Vatican and the Quirinale.

The inadequate size of the palace meant that only the closest members of James's household could be given accommodation. The rest, such as the Nithsdales, would be obliged to take lodgings elsewhere. William and Winifred travelled to Rome in the company of Lord Kilsyth, Lord Kingston and Mr Fleming, and after a few days at the Scots College, set about finding themselves rooms. They were all distressed by the high price of accommodation and decided to form themselves into small groups in one building so they could share their meals and only one cook need be employed.

The Nithsdales took rooms on the first floor of a building near the palace, with Charles Wogan and Mr Cameron above them and Lord Linlithgow and Mr Fleming below. The cook prepared a daily meal in the Nithsdales' kitchen and the cost was divided between them. Few people could afford proper suppers, and the majority made do with bread and wine. Most of the gentlemen then took themselves off to "a place like an English ordinary where everyone has his bottle of wine and anything else he calls for is apart".

James arranged that the Nithsdales and Mrs Hay, Murray's sister, should be given the use of his coach to explore the city "provided that they used it discreetly and did not spoil the horses". Butler, the king's coachman was to drive them and Sir William Ellis must always order it and was to "give it equally amongst them when they do not all go out together".

The Jacobites' reactions to the Holy City were mixed. Edgar, James's secretary, found it a place that "none could weary in", and was sure he would "wear out his shoes in a fortnight", while Mar, who was becoming more and more disillusioned with his life in exile, soon made up his mind that it was the "deadest town of so big a one he ever saw", and if it were not for the music in the churches and "some old Roman stones," he would not know what to do with himself.

Clemintina Sobieska (miniature Continental school)

CHAPTER 23

Marriage for James

While the captive Clementina was writing loving notes to James from Innsbruck, James was becoming tired of waiting for her. He was impatient to get his wedding over with, whoever ever his bride might be, and when he heard of an alternative princess, Maria Vittore di Caprara, he asked the Pope whether the proxy marriage that had taken place in Poland was legally binding. The Pontiff was not pleased with this enquiry and made it quite plain that James should continue to wait patiently for Clementina. James then wrote to Clementina telling her that she must try to escape and that he was sending an accomplice to help her. He dispatched Wogan forthwith to carry out this assignment but on his arrival in Olhau the young Irishman was at a loss to know how it should be done. "I wish I had Lady Nithsdale with me who is so good at these things," he wrote back.

Inspired by her initiative, he made his plans and completed the fairy story of Clementina's romance by engineering her escape from Innsbruck. His fellow conspirators were Mrs Misset, an Irish officer's wife, two of her friends and one of Mrs Misset's servants, a courageous girl named Jane, who had been persuaded to play a crucial part in the rescue by changing places with the imprisoned princess. Once in Innsbruck, they took rooms in the inn, pretending to be Clementina's relations who had come to pay her a visit. They managed to get a message to Clementina to inform her of their plans and she sent a secret reply that she was prepared to play her part.

That night they set out for the schloss taking Jane, wrapped in a thick cloak to protect her from the late winter snow. They presented her to the guards and sent a message to Clementina's mother, who sent down one of her gentlemen in waiting. He told the guards that the girl was his mistress and bribed them to let him take her in. Inside the castle, they went up to Clementina's room, where she had prepared herself for bed and dismissed her maids, telling them she wished to say her prayers.

Clementina then dressed herself in the thick clothes that she had made ready beforehand; a furred waistcoat over two flannel under-petticoats and an apron with four pockets to hold her possessions. Over this she wore a plain head-dress and a quilted cape, lined with rose-coloured silk. While Jane began to put on Clementina's night clothes and get into her bed, Clementina filled her pockets with as many of her belongings as she could and wrapped up her jewels in a piece of coarse linen. After she had embraced her mother for the last time, the gentleman in waiting led her out past the guards who were sheltering against the driving sleet. Wogan was waiting for her and took her to the inn where the others had made preparations to leave. They quickly got into the waiting Berlin and had only gone a few miles when Clementina remembered she had left her jewels behind her in the inn. They rushed back to collect them before setting off once more.

Ironically enough, while Clementina was making her daring escape across Europe to meet her future spouse, James had left Italy for Spain. Plans for the Spanish invasion had taken shape satisfactorily and an advance party had already set sail for Britain. The Duke of Ormonde had indicated that it was time for James to join them.

James had sent a final note of encouragement to Clementina: "When you are mine, I shall be happy, but, without you, greatness and the Crown itself will be a burden to me. Duty makes me seek them, but they will have no attraction for me unless you share them." He had left Rome quietly, keeping his destination secret from his compatriots. As a decoy he sent Mar, Perth and a small party in the direction of Innsbruck and fooled the English spies into thinking that he had gone in person to rescue Clementina. Mar, he hoped, would join him in Spain later.

Murray was left in charge of affairs while he was away. If Clementina were to arrive, he was to act as proxy at the wedding ceremony. Lady Nithsdale, Mrs Hay and the newly arrived Duchess of Mar were to wait on her. In the mean time they explored the town within the walls where horses were stabled on the ground floors of the shabby plastered houses, and herbs were grown in window boxes to freshen the air, as well as the gardens beyond where geraniums jasmine and oleander grew among the ancient ruins.

The Duchess of Mar, a sister of Lady Mary Wortley Montagu, was a bright, engaging creature who endeared herself to Winifred by loudly voicing her disapproval of Murray. Murray in his turn took every opportunity to discredit Mar. By this time Mar had made up his mind to leave James, and if he could not get a pardon from George, to go and settle with his wife in France.

When James arrived at Cadiz he found a disconsolate Ormonde waiting for him. Once again wild seas had dashed the Jacobite hopes. Although Earl Marischal had managed to land at Loch Alsh and set up their headquarters in Eilean Donan, the main part of the Spanish fleet who were to arrive with reinforcements had been severely damaged and forced to turn back. After a skirmish with government troops the Jacobites had been overcome and were making their way back to the Continent. James, doggedly refusing to give up hope of a second attempt, stayed on in Spain.

Meanwhile, after a journey hampered by bad weather which caused numerous halts and breakdowns, Clementina finally arrived incognito at Bologna. There she bought herself clothes and children's shoes for her tiny feet. When the Pope was informed of her arrival he sent the Papal Legate to greet her, bearing gifts: a looking glass and toilet boxes, posies and nosegays and the offer of a box at the opera. Though terrified of being recognised she felt obliged to attend and sat through the evening with her hood pulled well down over her face.

On 9th May she rose early, dressed her small figure in white, hung the famous Sobieski pearls round her neck and went to hear mass. Then, with James Murray who had arrived from Rome to act as proxy, bringing with him his sister Mrs Hay, she went through a simple wedding service. The next day the whole party set out for Rome in a cheerful mood. James was married and there was nothing the Hanoverians could do about it.

The Pope, delighted to hear of the princess's arrival, arranged for Clementina to be met at the Flaminian Gate outside the city by two cardinals, who conducted her to the Ursuline convent where beautiful apartments had been made ready for her at the Pope's expense, and where she was to stay until James returned. The following morning His Eminence sent her a regale of all sorts of refreshments carried by fifty-two men; Cardinal Gualterio presented her with a picture of James drawn by Penello de Treisano and Cardinal Aquaviva presented her with 20,000 pistoles in the name of the King of Spain. The same day, the cardinal held a congregation of ceremonials and it was decided that she should be treated with all the respect that was given to James. Later, she was received by the Pope with a great show of affection and full honours. After an hour's conversation she was given a magnificent collation and the Pope decreed that she should be styled Queen of England and should receive a pension equal to the one he had granted to James.

This triumphant welcome to Rome did little to prepare Clementina for the life of an exiled queen which was to come. She was also unaware of the altercation that was taking place amongst her courtiers. Murray's exalted position had gone to his head and he had begun to treat his fellow courtiers, even those senior to him in age and rank, with impertinence. He was determined to be spokesman for them all and told the Italians and other outsiders that his fellow Jacobites were poverty-stricken not only in their fortunes but in their heads. When Cardinal Aquaviva wanted to invite twenty of them to dinner he told him that only four Irishmen were fit to go.

With the arrival of Clementina in Rome, it was hoped that this unfortunate situation might change. At least Murray would be obliged to present them to the queen, or so they thought. After many promptings Murray agreed to do so, and told them to wait at the convent door the next day. They gathered there in anticipation until, finally, the door opened and their petite, fair-haired queen stood on the steps before them. As

Murray did not introduce them, they each went up and kissed her hand without her knowing who any of them were. As soon as this was over, Murray and his sister Mrs Hay led Clementina away to her carriage.

William and the senior lords were outraged, and lost no time in demanding to be introduced formally, requesting that the introductions should be made by someone of equal rank. Murray proposed that Wogan should make the introductions, whereupon William protested that he was treating them all like footmen and he would not tolerate his behaviour. However, when the others suggested going directly to the queen and explaining what was going on, William refused to do so, saying that she must not be upset and they must wait until James returned.

Winifred was enchanted by their young queen and wrote at once to Mary Traquair, "she is one of the charmingest, obliging and well bred ladies that ever was seen. Our master can but be extremely happy and all those who had the good fortune to have any dependence upon her. To add to it she is pretty, has good eyes and a fine skin, well shaped for her health but is not tall, but maybe yet, for she is but seventeen but looks younger."

It was all the more galling for Winifred and Lady Mar to realise that Murray was making sure that only his sister would become the queen's closest confidante. When they went out with her in her coach Mrs Hay always made sure to sit between them and Clementina. Fortunately Winifred had an ally in the Church. Neither Murray nor his sister were Catholics and the cardinals refused to allow Mrs Hay to stay with Clementina in the convent. Furious at hearing this, Murray wrote to James saying that Lady Nithsdale was in league with the Jesuits and that she was intent on staying in the convent and forcing herself on the queen.

James lingered on in Spain, hoping that another assault could be made later in the year, but Spain was faring badly in the war against England and France and needed all her resources on that front. She had lost ships, men and arms which were badly needed at home and interest in using James was waning. It finally became obvious that Spain would have to make her peace with England. There was nothing for it but for James to return to Italy and the bride who had been waiting patiently for him for the last six months.

Everyone was delighted to hear of their king's return and hoped that once he was married and settled in Rome, Murray would be put in his place. The first disappointment came when they were told that the wedding was to take place outside Rome in Montefiascone, a place so small that only a few of them would be invited to attend. The summer heats in Rome were the reason given for this but the Nithsdales

Clementina (engraving by Drevet, after Antonio David, Drambuie Collection).

and those left behind could not help feeling aggrieved as Clementina left for her wedding accompanied only by Mr and Mrs Hay, James Murray, and a small group of favourites. Lord Pitsligo felt obliged to write a long letter to his king recounting the resentment they all felt at Murray's behaviour. But James had greater worries on his mind.

He had written to Ormonde that they were "in a terrible way for money matters" and accused the Pope of being mean with them. He directed Dicconson as to how his meagre income could be spread over all the exiles. "The overplus of the arrears should be applied to the relief of those who would actually perish without such support, that all such as H.M. now subsists, whether old or new pensionable servants, should be able without distinction, supplied according to their different necessities, such only excepted as have pensions from the Court of France." He hoped that his servants would try to find employment elsewhere as he could now only look on them as "faithful suffering subjects whom he will supply with their fellow sufferers as far and as long as he is able". He asked that the "little chapel of crystal glass given by the Pope may be sold for the relief of our poor people".

Wedding of James and Clementina (Massuci, National Galleries of Scotland).

The arrival of the joyful Clementina and her suite was a welcome respite for the despondent king. The bronze gates of the city were by tradition always left open as a symbol that the bishop was perpetually ready to receive his master the Pope. Now he received the *de jure* king and queen of Britain with equal hospitality, having procured gifts of game and wine from the surrounding countryside. A lavish banquet was being prepared as the couple, who were to be married at midnight that evening, met for the first time.

For Clementina, who had suffered imprisonment and an exciting escape across Europe to meet her bridegroom, it was the culmination of a romantic adventure. Now at last she would be Queen of England. For James, whose *joie de vivre* had been extinguished by constant disappointment, she was one of the few aspirations in his life which came up to his expectation. The marriage ceremony was performed in an upstairs chapel of the cathedral, as if the proxy wedding had never taken place, and attended by the dignitaries of the town and the nobility of the district. After the extravagant banquet, the royal couple and their guests returned to the cathedral where the students of Montefiascone put on a theatrical performance in their honour.

A few days later James wrote to Ormonde, "it is no more my business now to publish the Queen's praises but to a friend with whom I have no reserve I cannot say but once and for all that she has surpassed my expectation and that I am happy with her".

James was delighted that Clementina had got on so well with Mr and Mrs Hay and James Murray. They were his closest friends and when he received Lord Pitsligo's letter he was unable to understand his point of view. He wrote a stiff letter back, giving no credence to any of the complaints.

CHAPTER 24

Birth of Prince Charles Edward

God Bless the royal heir
God Bless the Royal pair
Both King and Queen;
That from them we may see
A royal progeny
To all posterity
Ever to reign
JACOBITE ROYAL ANTHEM.

The establishment of the Jacobite court in Rome was a source of excitement for Roman society. The Muti Palace was an insignificant building of moderate size which stood at the end of a small cul-de-sac leading off the via del Corso, but what it lacked in palatial grandeur was compensated for by the uniformed Papal guard on duty night and day and the royal coat of arms which hung above the entrance. A few yards away stood the church of the Santi Apostoli, a large white Romanesque building, where the king and queen and Catholic exiles heard mass.

The tall, distinguished James and the radiant young queen were treated as royalty by Roman society. The queen was intelligent and beguiling and the king serious and dignified. They attended balls and operas and musical soirées, and visitors from Britain who watched them curiously from afar could not help contrasting this good-looking, civilised couple with their Hanoverian king at home.

While rejoicing in their master and mistresses's popularity, the Nithsdales themselves were far from satisfied. After receiving James's curt letter, not only Lord Pitsligo himself, but also several of James's most decent followers had left Rome without waiting for his return. As Winifred wrote, "I am the only one left of my station and shall in all appearances be yet more trampled on than we were both in our Master's absence."

William was in favour of leaving with the others but Winifred realised that financially this was impossible. She knew full well that only those who were receiving their jointures or other money from home could afford to live away from James's bounty. She also felt she had a good chance of being given the position of governess to Clementina's child if and when she had one. Clementina had written a friendly handwritten note to "ma cousine la comtesse de Nithsdale" from Montefiascone thanking her for her good wishes and expressing her happy assurance of seeing her when she returned to Rome.

To their regret, Murray was still James's right-hand man. His brother-in-law, John Hay, had been made Secretary of State and Mrs Hay was still permanently at Clementina's side. The Nithsdales resented the fact that they were obliged to live and eat most of their meals outside the palace while others who received the same pension as they did were lodged inside. They were required to wait upon their king and queen without any official duties being allotted to them and two or three times each day they had to walk from their lodgings to the Muti Palace to enquire whether they were needed. Winifred was often asked to accompany Clementina in her carriage or sit with her in her apartments but she always felt that the young queen had been poisoned against her and was keeping her distance.

The jealousies and quarrels in the Muti Palace were even more extreme than those at St Germain-en-Laye. In the words of Earl Marischal, "it was no place for an honest man". The court was smaller and further away from Britain, with less coming and going across the Channel, and the Pope was a poor subsitute for their former benefactor, King Louis, who had always kept their welfare at heart. Base plots and schemes were more rife here, and it had to be admitted that a deposed king trying to regain his crown had more prestige than the son of a deposed monarch who was hoping one day to become king.

Though James was conscientious to a fault in his wish to care for his people in a material way his natural detachment removed him from the mental torment caused by the day-to-day squabbles and jealousies that took place around him. He refused to allow Clementina, who had a more congenial, intuitive nature, to take any part in the management of the court.

Winifred had another problem on her hands. She knew that, as ever, William was living beyond his means and running up debts, and was mortified to learn that, without telling her, he had written to the Traquairs to ask for a loan. She at once wrote to Mary Traquair apologising. She confided to her sister-in-law that she could not understand how William managed to spend money so easily. They both received the same pension. They each paid thirty pistoles a meal, she paid for Evans' board and lodging and for some of Anne's education though, through the good offices of a cardinal, she had managed to get help from the Pope for this. William kept one servant for whom he only paid board and lodging, though the man constantly complained to Winifred that he had not received his wages. They had each bought one suit of clothes but she still wore her mourning, and although William paid for their lodgings, as she pointed out, they shared a bed so it would be no less if he were on his own. She was as depressed as she had ever been and poured out her heart to Mary, whom she looked on as her closest friend. Her letter ended: "I have reason to believe he would be very much better pleased if I were not with him for he then would be at his freedom to act as he pleased whereas now he is in some constraint, which I am sorry to put him to, since it has no other effect than of giving him trouble without benefit; whereas it is but the latter that I wish to be to him, and the first I would most willingly take upon myself to free him from it, if it were in my power."

Letter writing is no substitute for conversation. Mary Traquair could not understand the anguish that Winifred was going through and could only sympathise with her adored brother and his ruined life in exile. She wrote back to Winifred with a reprimand for having criticised William.

Winifred was bitterly hurt to receive Mary's letter and replied quickly, "since it has been taken so it shall never happen again and to any other person I would die before I would acquaint any living soul with my affairs of that kind, and hence forward will seek my comfort of any thing of that kind in God alone".

She was conscious that the Traquairs were of the opinion that her own family should give her more help. They had every reason to take this view, for her brother had now reclaimed his estates and was living once again at Powis Castle. But when Winifred had been desperate for clothes, not liking to appear in court in "nearly rags", she had written to his daughter, Mary Herbert, but had received no answer. Winifred sadly concluded that the great state her brother lived in was only to her disadvantage, for no one could imagine that she was in need when they thought that she had relations able to help her. But, as she said, "ability without will is of little use to me".

In March the following year she heard the news that she had been waiting for. The king told Winifred that Clementina was pregnant. She had heard the preganancy being discussed by Clementina's coterie for many weeks previously, but when Winifred made enquiries as to why Clementina was feeling unwell she had been told, both by the queen and by her ladies, that she only had a cold. Winifred resented the fact that Mrs Hay, who had never given birth herself, was the one who had been allowed to put her hand on the queen's stomach and "felt it stir" and was looking after the queen during her pregnancy. She felt gloomy about her prospects of obtaining the post of governess but, knowing that nothing is gained without asking, she approached James in a private interview asking if she might have the care of the "young lord or lady".

James agreed that, although she had all the qualities necessary for such a position, he had made up his mind to take no servants while he was abroad and would not appoint a governess. He concluded: "My wife has but little to do and will look to it herself. It is true she cannot always be there but when she is not Lady Misset will stay with it."

Baptism of Prince Charles Edward Stuart (Massuci, National Galleries of Scotland).

Winifred took this as another snub and felt she would "rather eat a crust in quiet and not be liable to the slights and mortifications I daily meet with". However, three reasons made her grit her teeth and stay on. The first was that, if they left the court, their pensions would be greatly reduced. The second was that should there be "an alteration in our Master's affairs and he returns home", they would be likely to receive more favour if they had stood by him. Lastly, by asking for nothing from the Terregles estate which Charles Traquair was now hoping to buy back from the government for their son, she would facilitate matters for him.

That summer she had heard from her sister, Mary, that Sir George had died and had not, as he had promised, made William his heir but had instead left everything to a cousin. Furthermore, he had taken £30,000 from his wife and left her with nothing but her jointure. Out of this she would have to pay £4000 worth of debts. Her husband, she now admitted, had been "very unjust to me both living and dying". Mary promised Winifred that she would not abandon young William but would "rather pinch" herself

than let him want "what be necessary for his education". Lord Nithsdale had made up his mind his that son should return to Scotland to start legal proceedings to claim back Terregles. Nothing would convince him that the debts had not been cleared. The Traquairs were not happy at the idea of William returning to Scotland for they had heard often enough of Jacobites, especially young men who could be suspected of spying, being put under arrest when they returned from abroad. They also thought that James should be consulted in case it was thought that the Nithsdales were conniving with the government. Added to this, they did not trust Mr Grant, the tutor that Sir George had provided and who would be travelling with him, and they doubted his loyalties both in politics and religion.

William made light of their worries. He was set on obtaining money from the estate and wrote to the Duke of Argyll recomending his son to his protection and asking his advice as to whether he should visit England or not. The Duke replied in the affirmative and accordingly William, accompanied by Mr Grant, set out for London. There they stayed with his aunt, Lady Montagu, and William was advised by his lawyer that he should appear before the court in Scotland or he would lose all claim to his estate.

In Scotland he was invited to stay with his uncle and aunt at Traquair. Both Linton and John had returned from abroad and the cousins enjoyed each other's company. Anne and Lucy, in spite of their education in France, were still unmarried though a younger sister, Mary, had just become engaged to a widower, Lord John Drummond, the younger brother of the Duke of Perth. However, it was the pretty, lively Catherine who caught William's eye.

The business side of his visit was less successful. He found that, as the Traquairs had told his father all along, the estate was still in the hands of creditors but he made a formal application that it should be returned to him. He was advised that, if he lived abroad as economically as possible for a few years, the estate would at last be free of creditors and he could take up residence there. Before he departed he was delighted to learn that Catherine reciprocated his love and was willing to wait for him.

In Rome, Clementina was treated with every care during her pregnancy. For the first few months she did not set foot outside the palace and was always carried up and down the marble stairs. When summer arrived she was transported in a chair into the garden where she was allowed to take a little exercise.

As the time for the birth drew near great preparations were made for the lying-in at the Muti Palace. James was determined that the birth should be witnessed by the most notable people in Rome and all his court were expected to be present, looking as well-dressed as possible. This was an acute problem for the Nithsdales. Winifred dared not decline to be present and likewise dared not appear in her old clothes.

Her dilemma was solved, she confided to Mary Traquair, when she managed to procure a handsome suit "through the good offices of a cardinal who had got it from the Pope, but that is between you and I for I was forbid to let it be known". William, as usual, wrote to his sister and asked for a "loan" of £50 to buy himself a new suit.

The great event took place on the last day of the year 1720 and was witnessed by a large crowd of onlookers. Prince Charles Edward Lewis Casimir Silvester Maria Stuart was born and straight away baptised in the adjoining chapel of Archetto. A royal salute was fired from the Castel Sant Angelo and the Pope presented the young prince with a useful gift of 10,000 scudi besides celebrating a mass in his honour. All across Europe Catholics rejoiced with fireworks, illuminations and fountains of wine. The Jacobites in England and Scotland celebrated as openly as they dared. The birth of the Stuart heir that George of Hanover had tried so hard to prevent had taken place after all.

CHAPTER 25

The Muti Palace

The Jacobites soon decided that their little prince was an infant prodgidy, while the Hanoverian spies reported that he was bandy-legged, delicate and unlikely to live. Winifred kept Mary Traquair up to date with every detail of his progress. It was one small way that she could return her debt to the Traquairs. At only two months he was "one of the finest children of his age ever to be seen" and was being suckled by an Italian wet nurse and was said to be showing signs of cutting teeth. This spectacular news had to be corrected six months later when she wrote, "I am sorry I cannot tell you that he has got some teeth for though he has often had what people judge to be symptoms of being about them, I could never perceive that there was any approaching ones till this day." She promised, "I shall not fail informing you when the first appears knowing how great a share you take in what regards him."

Muti Palace (drawn by Brian Vaughan).

The presence of the robust young Stuart prince in Rome was a perpetual threat to the British government. They regularly turned out propaganda which proclaimed that James was "old Mr Melancholy", his wife delicate and unable to have any more children and their son ailing. Those with a political career ahead of them felt it prudent to avoid Rome altogether and Lord Chesterfield advised his son that if he went there he should keep well away from the Pretender. Some of the cardinals and city officials wished that the Jacobites would leave the city altogether. Not only was it a great expense maintaining the Stuart king but his presence was preventing tourists from coming in.

When the more adventurous British visitors did pay their respects to James's court they were agreeably surprised by what they found. During the first years of their married life James and Clementina kept open house for anyone of importance who came from Britain and invited them to dine at their table where ten or twelve covers were set each day. British visitors were also astonished by how much at home they felt in the Muti Palace, for they found James took great care to live as much as possible in an "English" way, insisting on serving roast beef and ale in preference to Italian dishes and dressing his son in the British fashion. From his conversation it was noted that he was completely *au fait* with affairs in Britain and neither he nor his wife were the bigots that adverse propaganda maintained. They kept a Protestant chaplain and chapel for the large number of non-Catholics among his court.

Soon after the birth of Prince Charles, the British government appointed an official spy, Baron Philip von Stosch, who worked as an art and antique dealer in Rome. Stosch soon controlled a large network of spies and handed out money to informers, writing regular letters home reporting every movement in the Muti Palace. When James's finances were particularly low and his servants were late in receiving their wages, Stosch reported that even "the tapestries in the room spoke". At times he was given so much information that he was unable to pay for it all and insisted that either the government must allow the exiled Jacobites to get money through from Britain more easily, or he, Stosch, must have his pay increased. The baron was a great believer in the power of wine to open mouths and referred to it as the "la clef universelle des mysteres humains". But sometimes food was equally useful and, during the course of lengthy dinners, small pieces of information about future Jacobite plans were bound to slip out.

The Jacobites did not take long to find out exactly who "John Walton" was. They were as adept at intercepting letters as the government and they played an equally cunning game by visiting Stosch and feeding him false pieces of information. John Hay, curious to know how he would deal with such a request, went to see him on the pretext of buying a work of art and, while making conversation, insinuated that he was tired of working for James and was looking for a pardon. But the baron was not fooled and refused to fall into the trap.

Meanwhile the Jacobites in Britain tried to keep up both their own spirits and those of their friends abroad with defamatory gossip about King George. His dislike of his son, the Prince of Wales, was good grist for the mill and they encouraged the rumour that George did not believe himself to be the prince's father. George's debaucheries were also reported with glee. Gifts such as a snuff box decorated with the famous incident when his four-poster bed collapsed as he made love to his mistress, were widely distributed.

It was unfortunately becoming apparent that the Stuart king and queen were also experiencing difficulties in their marriage, though in their case it was a clash of personalities rather than infidelity which was the cause. Clementina had a mercurial temperament. She was intelligent and capable but could throw a fit of temper when she did not get her own way. She had a passionate nature and expected more from her husband than a distant fatherly relationship. James never shared any of his affairs of state with her and she was often under the impression that everyone else in the palace knew more than she did. Quarrels began to break out between the couple and, the more temperamental Clementina became, the more dictatorial James became towards her. Unable to receive the affection she craved from her husband, Clementina became obsessively attached to her women companions and they were not slow in making use of their position and influence.

Winifred observed the goings on at court without comment but still reported back every detail about the prince. He was "little for his age" but was "lively enough". He was weaned "with so little trouble that it has not caused him an ill night. The wet nurse put alloe on her nipple and after he tasted it once he could never look at her breast again." By May he had a very good appetite, still could not stand or walk but was in very good health and every day he grew "more charming". The queen, she added, was still not "abreeding".

To assist her breeding, and to take a short respite from the Muti Palace, Clementina decided to spend a month in Bagnio di Lucca, famous as a place of pilgrimage as well as for its hot baths. She took only Mrs Hay with her, but was later joined by James. While he was in Lucca, Clementina watched him performing the ceremony of touching for the King's Evil, or Scrofula. After the priest had finished reading the gospel, the king, who had been kneeling, surrounded by the sick children, sat down. A gentleman of the bed chamber brought each child to him in turn and with his joined hands he touched them on both cheeks. He then hung round their neck a medallion with Saint Edward on one side and on the other, three sailing ships. His manner "radiated holiness, so great was the earnestness of spirit which he showed, and the gentleness of his movements".

When the king and queen returned to Rome they appeared to be on more amicable terms. As other courtiers came and went, James began to realise that the Nithsdales were steadfast in their loyalty and began to appreciate their constancy. On their wedding anniversary that year he and Clementina dined with them and "were so obliging as to be truly merry".

Touchpiece (National Museums of Scotland).

In the autumn of the same year William confessed he was seriously in debt. He had drawn a bill for £150 and if it was not honoured within three weeks they would be ruined. William had already written to his sister for help but now he implored Winifred to do the same. Though driven frantic by his extravagance she could refuse him nothing and, knowing the shame that would face them if the bill could not be met, she put pen to paper and tried to explain the circumstances to Mary Traquair. "When I see him in difficulties which is not in my power to relieve, it goes to my heart", she wrote. She pleaded a second time that the furniture could be sold. When no answer came immediately she wrote again in desperation. She had to borrow money or they would be turned out of their lodgings. "I beg of you, by all that is dear to you, to have compassion on us for if this fails and we were starving none would let us have a sixpence." She explained that they had pawned all their credit to hinder their being molested until the bill could be answered. "If the bill is protested " she continued, "I have reason to fear that [Lord Nithsdale] will be in a more shameful confinement than his last."

The Traquairs again came to the rescue and Winifred asked Mary to get Father Hudson to write to William and tell him that he must no longer be a drain on them. She confessed that she herself had absolutely no influence on him. If Father Hudson did write it had no effect, for only a few months later William wrote to Traquair saying that, unless he could procure another £100 a year to make himself "easy", they would both have to leave the court. He found it impossible to dress himself on their pension and if they were not well dressed they were criticised by their companions for disgracing the whole court. He maintained that most of the others whose estates were forfeited were now having them administered by relations who could send them money. The fact that his estate was nearly bankrupt seemed to have escaped him. He adds "death and sickness and necessary absence makes it that there is none of my rank to appear in public with my master, which makes it a greater difficulty for me to remove".

For once, Mary resisted her brother's request. She pointed out that if he did manage to procure another £100 a year, he would only after a short time decide that he needed another £100, so he should try to manage on what he had. William then took the unforgivable step of approaching James and giving him the impression that the Traquairs were in some way preventing him from getting possession of his estate. He said that he had never been told whether the estate was in the hands of the government or the creditors, nor to whom the rents were being paid. This prompted James to write a formal letter to the Traquairs asking them if they would satisfy Lord Nithsdale in this matter.

The letter could not have arrived at a worse time. A few days after receiving it Charles Traquair was taken so seriously ill that he was given the last sacraments and bade farewell to his wife and children. Mary could not help feeling that the shock of receiving the letter had contributed to his illness. At last she was able to sympathise with Winifred and wrote back to her brother telling him how hurt she was and that she considered it "a sad return for all the favours my husband has done before and since you went abroad he had honoured your bills and supplied your wants without a scrape of the pen from you beside the considerable sum you owed him formerly". They were naturally particularly upset that he should have given "one we value so infinitely as we do Sir John" (pseudonym for James) a completely false impression about their affairs. She enclosed papers which demonstrated that her husband had no management of Terregles, that it had been in government hands until November 23rd of that year and on that day his life rent had been bought (to a great advantage as everyone thought) on behalf of creditors. She added that Charles Traquair had paid an English lawyer for an appeal in case the matter had to come before Parliament.

Winifred was, as usual, humiliated by her husband's behaviour and her relationship with the Traquairs was only resumed after some months.

Prince Henry (by David, National Galleries of Scotland)

CHAPTER 26

Birth of Prince Henry

The birth of "another brave boy" to Clementina on 6th March 1725, was heralded with more fanfares across Europe and gave the impression that the Chevalier and his young wife were still in a state of married bliss. This, unfortunately, was far from being the case.

In spite of James having taken every precaution in the appointment of a nurse for Prince Charles, his first choice, Mrs Henry, had been found dabbling in political intrigue and had had to be instantly dismissed. While Clementina had been pregnant with her second baby, Mrs Hay, to whom she was still devoted, had been forced to return to England to settle up her family affairs and, while there, had been accused of spying and had been put into Newgate prison. Clementina, desperate that she should be present at this birth as she had been at the last, had tried unsuccessfully to pull every string possible for her release. James had found another nurse for Charles, a devout Catholic named Mrs Sheldon, and she offered to look after Clementina when the time came. After Prince Henry's birth the two women became very attached to each other.

Either because he was jealous of this close friendship or because of his permanent fear of being accused of bigotry, James, without consulting Clementina, suddenly dismissed Mrs Sheldon from his service, his explanation being that "Prince Charles was getting among servants where children never learn any good" and it was time that he was put among men. He then recalled James Murray, whom he had created Earl of Dunbar, and made him the prince's governor.

Clementina was furious on two accounts; firstly the high handed manner in which James had acted, and secondly because, although Mrs Hay had now returned, she maintained that she wanted a Catholic governor for her child. Previously she had never been at all bigoted and had told a visitor that the prince was likely to live and die amongst Protestants and that in her country there were no distinctions except between the honest and the dishonest. Mrs Sheldon was firmly behind her and the court were not happy at the reappearance of James Murray to add to the fray.

An almighty row broke out, which ended in Clementina accusing James of having an affair with Mrs Hay and refusing to be mollified until he dismissed both the Hays from the court.

James was quite unable to deal with her tantrums and resorted to writing notes imploring her to "return to reason, to duty to yourself and to me, who await your submission with open arms, to restore you to peace and happiness".

Winifred, like the other members of the household, witnessed endless sulks and scenes on the part of Clementina and pained, long-suffering silences on the part of James. Submission was the last thing Clementina intended and she finally issued an ultimatum. Unless the Hays were dismissed she herself would leave.

To the astonishment of the court she was as good as her word. One morning she ordered her coach and demanded to be taken to the Convent of St Cecilia. Mrs Sheldon, who accompanied her, entered another in the Tor de Spechi. Shocked and hurt by the humiliation, James found that not only most of Roman society, but also the Pope himself took her side. A bishop was sent round to chastise James on his adultery and the Pope made it known that his pension would be withheld till further notice.

No one who knew James could seriously believe these accusations but Hanoverians were cock-a-hoop that the pure Stuart king had at last been involved in a scandal. The story of this affair spread like lightning and lingered on for some time in many varying versions. When Lady Mary Wortley Montagu travelled to Rome years later she wrote to her husband that she had at last discovered the "real" reason for Clementina's retreat into a convent. She had had an affair with the Pope and had taken refuge in the convent where she had intended to taker her life.

In her new position, Clementina soon found out that she was more powerful than she had ever been in the palace. The intriguing Cardinal Alberoni, the former advisor to the Spanish king, had fallen out with Spain and retired to Rome. He visited Clementina, supported her in her grievances and helped her to write to all her many influential relations, explaining that it was her religious zeal that had caused her to separate from her husband. The Pope showed his approval of her stand for her faith by withholding some of James's pension and adding to hers. She issued orders to her staff at the Muti Palace and demanded that her children were brought to see her. Winifred became accustomed to receiving several contradictory orders each day from her capricious mistress. Though he granted her all her petty wishes, James was firmly resolved to stand his ground on the main issue and refused to dismiss the Hays.

While Winifred was involved in this drama, she received a letter from the Augustine nuns at Le Fosse St Victoire to say that they could no longer educate her daughter Anne, as no fees had been paid for the last year. Lady Carrington had lost the remains of her fortune in the crash of the Mississippi Bank and could no longer support her niece. Since they had parted in France six years earlier Winifred had kept in close touch with Mrs Lindsay and she had sent her back detailed reports of their doings. Linton,

Lady Anne Maxwell.

who was Anne's godfather, had always taken his responsiblities seriously and Anne, who was a coquettish little girl, had enjoyed kneeling down and asking him for his blessing, whereupon Linton would blush shyly and say "God Bless you". When he had grown into a more sophisticated young man and had acquired a coach, he lent it to them to return their visits. Sitting up in Lord Linton's coach, dressed in their best, they would drive across Paris making their calls. All were described by Mrs Lindsay. "Prince Legre, the great Shalimar, and Mrs Law's daughter, although I put her last she is the richest .. ."

Knowing that Anne must remain in the convent as there was nowhere else for her to go, and not wanting to ask James directly as he had already arranged for the Pope to give her a sum towards Anne's education in the past, she decided to write to Mar in France, who she knew still had the ear of the king, and ask him to approach James on her behalf. "The king cannot do a greater act of charity" she wrote, if he could arrange for her daughter's education to be paid. James agreed to cover Anne's fees for another year but she knew she could not ask him to do so again.

The following autumn James decided to move some of his court temporarily to Bologna. He was anxious to move his children out of the Papal City and away from the prying eyes of Roman society. He would also be able to live there more economically on his reduced Papal pension. Lady Nithsdale was to accompany the two princes and Lord Nithsdale was to remain in Rome where he would wait on the queen. The Pope asked to see Prince Charles before he was removed from his city. He took him into the Vatican garden and tested him on his catechism, but the prince was shy and the Pope stated that he was not altogether satisfied with his religious education.

Before leaving, James paid his wife a final visit and asked her to accompany him. She remained firm that until the Hays were dismissed she would not leave the convent. James patiently accepted her decision. If only, as the Duke of Beaufort remarked, he had "taken her in his arms and carried her into his coach she would not have resisted". But such a gesture was not in James's character.

Winifred was delighted to have a respite away from her demanding mistress and felt, like many of the other women in the palace, that once Clementina was separated from her children she would be more eager to join her family. She also realised that at last she was being given unofficial responsibility for the care of Henry, the "little Duke".

James had travelled ahead to Bologna to choose their accommodation and Winifred followed with the two little princes who "agreed mighty well with the journey and they were much improved in health since they left Rome".

The palace lay outside the town surrounded by a large garden and everyone who joined them there felt relieved to be out of Rome and happier for the move. Two little ponies were brought from Sardinia and Charles trotted happily around the grounds, where his horsemanship was much admired.

While James Murray (Lord Dunbar) was responsible for Charles's education, Winifred made sure that his religious instruction was not wanting. Murray had mellowed over the years and the friction at court had brought the remaining courtiers together. Winifred and he had now settled into a comfortable relationship.

During the winter season the town of Bologna was a perpetual whirl of balls and dinners and, as John Hay discovered when he made a visit, it was "a place of much more diversion than Rome". James revelled in the company of his two small sons and allowed Charles to accompany him to many of the social events. The little prince's seventh birthday was celebrated by a magnificent ball given in the Casa Marescotti. The jewels of the ladies glinted in the candlelight of the spectacular candelabra and the *de jure* king and his heir were the focus of attention for the adoring Bolognese society.

During the Mardi Gras festivities, even the toddler Prince Henry, escorted by Winifred, made an appearance at the Casa Fibbia where another lavish ball was held. The nobility of Bologna were lost in admiration for the two delightful princes, dressed in tartan suits specially ordered from Scotland.

Later that spring it was known that George I was failing fast. Wishful thinking made the Jacobites hope that many of his statesmen would not be employed by his son, the Prince of Wales, and would consider coming over to the Jacobite side. Approaches were even made to Walpole, the Prime Minister, but he remained non-committal. The Emperor, however, was making noises in their direction and, if he gave them support, Spain could also be won over. But while Clementina remained separated from James no help would be forthcoming from either quarter. Pressure was mounting from Jacobites all over Europe for James to dismiss the Hays.The loyal John Hay (Lord Inverness) had written to Clementina as soon as she had left the palace saying that he was "ready to sacrifice everything that is dearest to me for your satisfaction to make your union with the king flourish", but James had obstinately refused to let them go. They were not only his close friends but John Hay was an important adviser. By April, however, he knew that he must accept his resignation, and the couple left Rome to go and live in Pisa.

When Clementina heard the news of their departure she merely remarked that "that was something but not all". It did, in any case, pacify the foreign powers who had taken her side and the Pope restored to James three-fifths of his pension, while giving the rest to Clementina direct. This particularly annoyed her husband, who could not understand why she was accepting money she did not need while he was in his usual straits. James was again asked by the Pontiff to bring Prince Charles to see him, so the little boy travelled to Rome with his father and was again tested on his catechism. This time, after Winifred's coaching, he answered perfectly and made a far better impression. James felt he had gained the point that a Protestant governor was no hindrance to the child's religious education.

The following winter James bought the Villa Almandine, a charming house in the countryside near Bologna, and here Lady Nithsdale and the princes and a nucleus of the court settled in. It was hoped that Clementina might now soon come and join them.

Prince Charles Edward (Antonio David, Drambuie Collection).

CHAPTER 27

Bologna

The news of King George I's death reached Bologna in the summer of 1727. His unfortunate wife, Sophie-Dorothea, who had, under his orders, spent most of her married life imprisoned in a castle in north Germany, had died before him, leaving a letter which summoned her husband to meet her before the judgement of God. On his last visit home George had been handed this dark message and had succumbed to the rendez vous the very same day.

James immediately recalled John Hay from Pisa and together they travelled to Lorraine to be closer to Britain. At the same time negotiations were reopened with Spain, to plan another landing. Before he left, James gave his official seal to the Nithsdales' appointments. Lord Nithsdale was to be head of the queen's family and was to stay on in Rome. There were signs that Clementina might at last be thinking of leaving the convent and, if this was the case, it would be Lord Nithsdale's delicate task to escort her to Bologna. His duties were detailed accordingly. "Lord Nithsdale will attend the Queen wherever she goes, will give her his hand, present people to her when she is out of her Bed Chamber, and give such orders as are to be given to the two Italian gentlemen. Every first day of the month Sir William Ellis will give the Queen a thousand livres for pin-money." The Queen was to have five courses served, dinner and supper, and six people should sit at her table.

Winifred's appointment ran as follows: "Our will and pleasure is that you forthwith swear and admit Our Right Trusty and Right well beloved Winifred Countess of Nithsdale into the place and quality of governess of our dearly beloved son Henry Duke of York. To have and to hold the said place with all the offices salaries perquisites and advantages there unto belongs. Given at our court at Bologna this 4th day of July 1727. In the 26th year of our reign. Signed James R."

Winifred sent James constant reports on his children's progress and health and their doting father was interested in every detail. When she told him that the Duke had cut two more teeth, he replied, "the Duke had twenty teeth when I left him so I can't comprehend how he can have any more, but if he should, he is strong and I hope he will bear it."

Clementina was at last making preparations to leave the convent and join her family. James hoped that Lord Nithsdale would first escort her to Bologna and then bring her to join him in Lorraine where he intended to spend the winter. The children were to stay safely in Bologna with Winifred as he considered the duke too young to make the journey and did not want the two brothers to be separated.

Before Clementina actually left the convent, Britain once again leant heavily on the Duke of Lorraine to deny James his hospitality and was he was obliged to take refuge once more in Avignon. When the news of his enforced removal was heard in England, a Member of Parliament commented in the House that it put him in mind of Charles II who, in his banishment, had been made to move so many times that he finally moved himself back to England.

In James's case, the removal back to England seemed to be ever less likely. George II had succeeded to his father's throne with little opposition. He had been wise enough to retain Walpole and most of his father's old ministers so they had no cause to defect to the Jacobite side. The Jacobites in Britain were not optimistic and Spain was reluctant to commit herself.

James still wished to remain in Avignon for a while in case the situation should change and he remade his plans for Clementina to join him there. To Winifred he wrote, "though I am persuaded nothing can be added to your zeal for me and my family, yet I am sure you will redouble, if possible, your care of the Duke, now that neither the Queen nor I will be with him, and I am entirely at ease about him, for that reason."

At the Villa Almandine, instructions were received daily for the packing and removal of those who were going to Avignon, and the dismissal and re-employment of others who would no longer be needed. The books were to be taken out of the chest and well packed so they would not suffer on the road, and sent with the plate. Deselle, the barber, was ordered to pack up the king's clothes and body linen with his toilette and send them over "in the cheapest manner". Apart from some wine which must be reserved for the children's household, and some that must be given as gifts, the remainder must be sold. He intended to live with the greatest frugality during the winter and wished the queen's journey to be conducted with the minimum of expense except when "the Queen's satisfaction and convenience are immediately concerned".

While these instructions were in the process of being carried out, William sent word that Clementina had left the convent and that they were setting out for Bologna. He also warned them that she was defiantly bringing Mrs Sheldon with her.

Clementina holding a mirror to emphasise her position as an uncrowned queen.

When the queen's party arrived at one o'clock in the morning, the whole household was up and ready to receive her. Murray had tactfully made an excuse to leave the court so that his presence would not annoy her and everyone else was on tenterhooks lest the smallest aggravation might cause her to return to the convent.

Clementina settled herself into her apartments and, being well aware of the advantage she had gained, she soon began to question all the instructions left by her husband. Lord Nithsdale found himself going backwards and forwards with messages to Sir William Ellis countermanding James's orders. Sir William would then write urgent letters to James asking whose orders they were to follow.

On the first day of every month Sir William had been authorised to pay the queen a thousand livres for "pin money". When she asked what this was supposed to cover she was told it was for her "tea, coffee, chocolate, the postage of her letters and all other personal expenses". It may have been in a fit of pique that she ordered "50 mils epingles" to be sent from London.

Negotiations were under way with the French to allow her to travel through France on her way to Avignon. To keep the British happy it was to be given out publicly that she was not to be allowed into the country though James was quietly assured that she would not be stopped.

Clementina listened impassively to the plans that were being made for her departure until they were at an advanced stage, when she suddenly announced that she had decided not to go but would prefer to remain at Bologna. Having already been made a prisoner on one journey across Europe she was not eager to make another, especially when France was loudly proclaiming that she would not be allowed through. She was also, once again, enjoying the company of her children who had been disciplined by Winifred to treat her carefully. Charles, who was a lively boy, had promised that he would not "jump near Mama".

James blamed the Pope for her refusal to travel, never having trusted him since he had chosen to support Clementina against him. He wrote to Sir William Ellis and told him to try any ruse to get her to change her mind, even to the extent of allowing her to bring Mrs Sheldon. He would, he said, dismiss her on arrival but "the main object is to get her here". When forced to accept the fact that Clementina was determined to stay where she was, he wrote to Murray that, sad though he was, he might be able to "draw advantage from it some other way".

The household in Bologna regretfully prepared themselves for a winter with their queen. William, now a man of fifty, found himself perpetually scurrying backwards and forwards with messages and complaints to Sir William Ellis from the twenty-five-year-old Clementina. It was a relief to him that much of her time was spent in her apartments with Mrs Sheldon, where their religious devotions took up a large part of the day.

The following January, James decided to leave Avignon. Fortunately Clementina had become very close to a nun in the Convent of St Pietro Martire in Bologna, who was an intelligent woman and had the sensible idea of inviting Mrs Sheldon to come and live in her convent. This she did and remained there until her death.

To the relief of the household a happy reconciliation appeared to take place between their king and queen though each of them had decided to lead their own life. Clementina devoted herself entirely to her religion, while James, when not at his desk, enjoyed the social life in Bologna. Though sad that his beautiful wife did not accompany him to the balls and dinners, he was comforted by the young Bolognese women who eagerly sought his company. Hanoverian spies constantly reported his liaisons with other women but no evidence was produced to support the rumours.

In spring there was general satisfaction when Clementina announced that she was pregnant. James was delighted, and so sure that it would be another boy that he planned to name him James and wrote to Clementina's father, Prince James Sobieski, to ask whether he would stand godfather. Winifred was put in charge of ordering the trousseau and preparing a nursery for the baby. When she wished to order a new cradle, she was told that the old one in Rome could easily be fitted up. She was allowed to order a new layette which included "caps of fine cambric edged with Flanders lace, nightcaps of the finest Holland with Flanders lace, satten mantles and caps and cambric gloves".

In the early months of her pregnancy, Clementina was involved in a slight accident when a curtain rod fell from above a window and hit her on the head. She was only slightly hurt but it was thought that the shock caused her to miscarry. Whether she was not fully aware of what had happened, or whether her usual desire to be enigmatic prevented her from announcing the fact is not known, but no one was informed. As time went on doubts were gradually expressed over the expected birth and it was generally held by the court that she had never been pregnant and that it had only been another sign of her hysterical disposition.

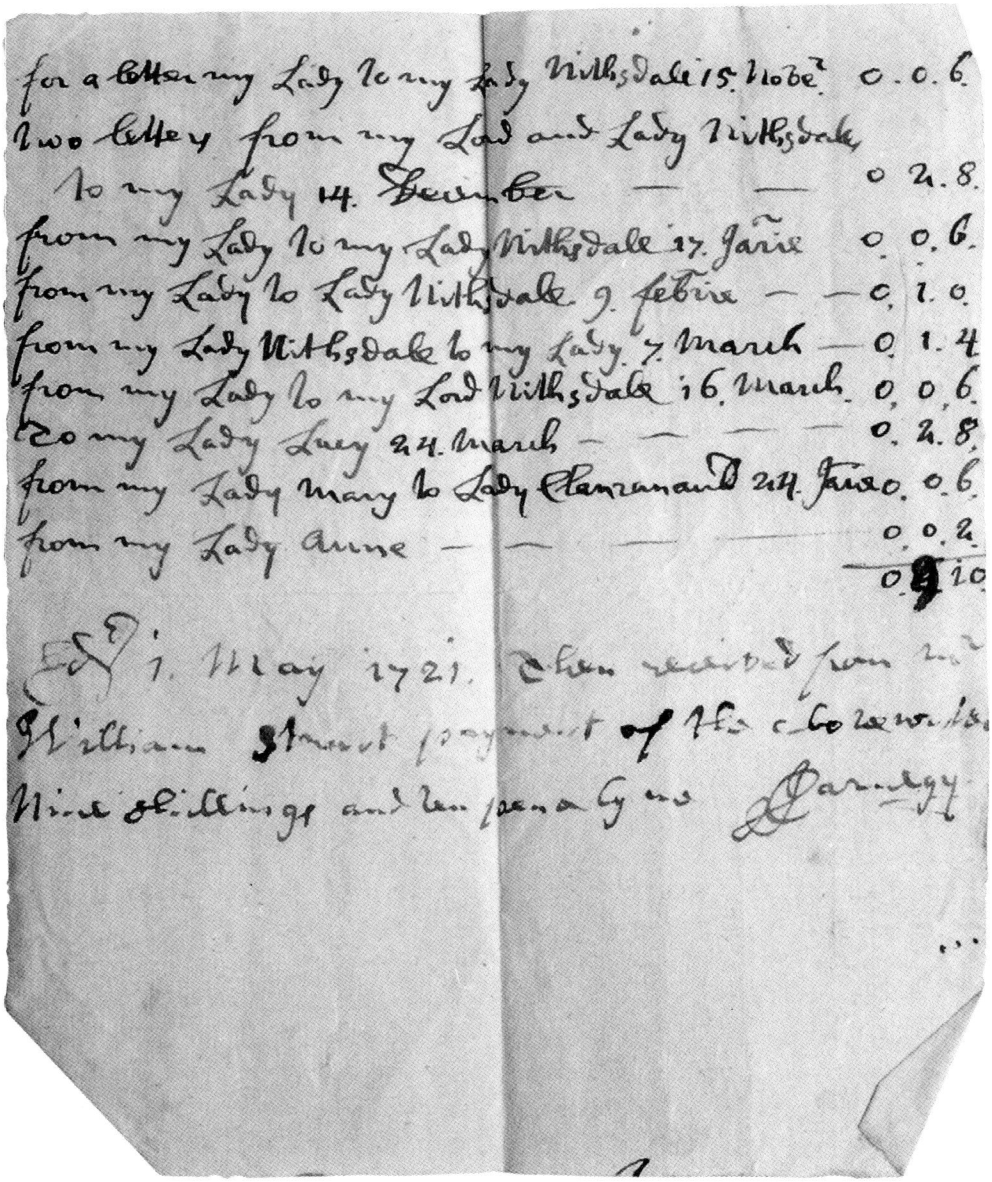

for a letter my Lady to my Lady Nithsdale 15. Nobr 0.0.6
Two letters from my Lord and Lady Nithsdale
to my Lady 14. December — — 0.2.8
from my Lady to my Lady Nithsdale 17. Janie 0.0.6
from my Lady to Lady Nithsdale 9. febrie — — 0.1.0
from my Lady Nithsdale to my Lady 7. March — 0.1.4
from my Lady to my Lord Nithsdale 16. March 0.0.6
to my Lady Lucy 24. March — — — — 0.2.8
from my Lady Mary to Lady Clanranald 24. Junie 0.0.6
from my Lady Anne — — — 0.0.2
0.9.10

Edr 1. May 1721. Then received from Mr
William Stuart payment of the above written
Nine shillings and ten pennys by me J Carnegy

Bill from Father Carnegie for carrying letters to and from France.

CHAPTER 28

A Husband for Anne Maxwell

In the spring of 1729 James decided that the whole court should return to Rome and Winifred realised that her time as governess was coming to an end. Prince Henry was four years old and of an age "to be put among men" and Mr Stafford, his new governor, had already arrived from Paris.

A few months previously Winifred had received a letter from her sister Anne Carrington saying that she was now nearly destitute and had not "a rag of clothes but what had been given out of charity". However, not discouraged, she was going to Spain to involve herself in mineral speculation. She could therefore no longer be responsible for Winifred's daughter Anne and Mrs Lindsay. Anne had grown into an attractive, dark-haired girl of eighteen and had completed her education so Winifred was obliged to ask James if Anne and her nurse could join her for a while in the Villa Almandine. She knew that she could not presume on the king's hospitality for long and also realised that the only way she could secure any kind of satisfactory future for her daughter would be to find her a husband.

James and his household went on ahead to Rome and Clementina and the children lingered on at the villa for a few months longer. When orders came for their removal James told Winifred to have a "suit of men's clothes" made for the duke to wear on his arrival in Rome. He confessed that he was impatient to see "Harry in his breeches". He also considered that it was high time for Carluccio, now eight, to resume his studies with his governor, Murray, who was about to return to Rome.

At the end of April, Prince Charles set off for Rome with his under-governor, Sir Thomas Sheridan, and James had given orders that Anne might be allowed to accompany them. A few weeks later the queen and the rest of the household followed. The queen sat with Henry on her knee and delighted the small crowd who watched their departure by kissing his hands and calling out "Ringrazzio ringrazzio".

On their return to Rome the Nithsdales still received their pensions and were expected at court but their duties were greatly reduced. Winifred was able to devote her time to making enquiries about eligible young men for Anne. She was not happy for her to be living in the shadows of the Muti Palace where many adventurers and undesirable characters turned up and spun stories which might easily capture the imagination of a young girl.

Anne had been brought up to know that her parents would find her a husband and she was also well aware that, as a Catholic and Jacobite with only the promise of a dowry that her brother might provide for her, she was not a great catch. She was twenty before a suitable husband had been chosen and eventually her parents had to consider a young man who was not of their faith.

Their choice was the twenty-nine-year-old John, Lord Bellew. His Irish father had been outlawed after his brother had fought for James II in Ireland and he had gone live in England, where he had become a Protestant and put down roots sufficiently to become a Member of Parliament. He had died in 1715, when John had succeeded to the title.

John Bellew remembered seeing Anne in Paris where she had made a great impression on him but she had no recollection of him. Extensive enquiries were made into his character which all proved favourable and he was invited to write to Lord Nithsdale asking for his daughter's hand in marriage. He too had been making enquiries, for he wrote to say that he "proposed to be entirely happie in the possession of the lady who had so fine a character with all those that know her and that he had conserved a perfect esteem for her since the time he had seen her". He confessed that he was not the possessor of a large income, though he had hopes of laying hands on some of the family's forfeited property in Ireland. The settlement he proposed to make on Anne seemed generous enough and it was settled that the marriage should take place at Lucca the following September. The journey there would be too expensive for two of them to go so only William escorted his daughter to her wedding.

Both the Nithsdales' children were married that year - for the previous June their son, William, was finally able to marry his cousin Catherine, who had waited for him despite being courted by another suitor. They had been married on 27th June, Lord Nithsdale's birthday, and had at last been able to return to Terregles. Winifred had at once written to Mary Traquair saying how happy she was that her son was "settled so much to his satisfaction" and hoped that he would make it his study to "make Lady Catherine happy also". Their satisfaction was only marred by the fact that William neglected to write and tell them that the wedding had taken place. His father was particularly annoyed and was not appeased by the fact that his son had inherited his own reluctance to write letters.

Six months after the wedding Lord Bellew was also trying to obtain an answer from William in Scotland. Anne had written to inform her brother of her marriage and had received no answer. Lord Bellew then wrote to ask when he intended to pay his sister's portion. He had, he said, made a special journey to Rome on the expectation of receiving it but as there had been nothing waiting for him and the expense of the journey had been great, he had been obliged to draw on him for 300.

This drew a response, and after some wrangling when John Bellew threatened to make William pay his wife's portion with interest from the time she was fifteen, it was agreed that a lump sum would suffice.

The following year both the Nithsdales and the Traquairs were made grandparents, the Nithsdales being grandparents twice over. Both young couples produced baby girls. The Bellews named their child Frances and the Maxwell's called their daughter Mary, after Mary Traquair.

Now that Anne's education was paid for Winifred was, for the first time, in a position to give gifts instead of always receiving them. She had always felt that she owed a great debt of gratitude to Lucy and the nuns at the English Convent in Bruges who had looked after her so well in her illness. With the strong organising ability shared by all the Herbert sisters, Lucy had decided to have a new chapel built for the nuns. A great part of their devotional life was spent in singing plain chant, and she had decided that a larger chapel with a dome would aid their devotions and magnify their soft voices. Winifred was commissioned to choose an altar in Rome and eventually a magnificent altar made from "crusted marble" - thin pieces of many different kinds of marble laid on stone - was dis-patched to Bruges. Later, to celebrate Lucy's jubilee, she sent each of the nuns "a pair of beads trimmed with a brass crucifix and a box in which was fourteen pictures of the passion, stiled the stations of the holy cross, to which great indulgences is given." This was the begining of the devotion to the Stations of the Cross which was being popularised by a Franciscan monk, Father Leonard of Port Maurice, (later to be canonised) who had made a great impression on both Clementina and Winifred. On this occasion Winifred also sent her sister the length of fine Flanders lace which had trimmed Prince James Edward's cradle and which had been given to her by Queen Mary Beatrice.

As Winifred had both the ear of the cardinals and of James she often found herself dealing with requests. One of these came from her sister Anne who complained that she and her niece were finding it difficult to obtain mineral rights in Spain because their titles were not considered good enough. Would Winifred, she pleaded, ask James to make her niece a Duchess? She confessed to being "a little piqued" when this request was refused.

Another was from a lady who enclosed a small, dried-up, cancerous growth. She sent it as proof of King James II's sanctity, for when she had discovered that she had a cancer in her breast she touched it with a piece of cloth that had spot of King James's blood on it. It had increased in size and finally her flesh had opened and the cancer had ejected itself. Ever since she had been perfectly well. She wished to send this as evidence for King James's canonisation.

The Nithsdales had now earned themselves not only the respect, but also the affection of James and their shared religion had helped them to come to terms with Clementina. Since their return to Rome she had become a member of the third order of the Dominicans and was devoting herself entirely to her religion and good works. Father Leonard had also encouraged her to conduct a mission among her friends and when possible to live as simply as she could. It was a relief to the impoverished exiles when she led a fashion for wearing plainer clothes at court. Though visitors found her charming, "friendly compassionate and charitable and her piety exemplary without bigotry," she and James were not compatible. Like his father he was growing old before his time, and was constantly taking cures for his various ailments. Their only point of contact was their religion and their mutual love for their sons.

CHAPTER 29

Two Deaths

The year 1735 opened with the death of Clementina at the pathetically early age of thirty-three. Her religious disciplines and penances had disguised the fact that she had been suffering from tuberculosis and she had gradually been devastated by the disease - one which had also attacked many of her family.

The Pope ordered that her emaciated body be given a royal funeral. Clothed in purple and velvet she lay for three days in her coffin on a magnificent catafalque in the Church of the Sancti Apostoli surrounded by hundreds of flickering wax tapers, watched over by two Dominicans and guarded by a royal escort of Papal guards with drawn swords. Her coffin was then solemnly processed to St Peter's by thirty-two cardinals and there, in the great basilica draped in black, a solemn funeral service was held. According to her wishes, before her body was finally interred in the crypt below, she was taken out of her royal robes and dressed instead in the plain white habit of the Dominican third order.

She left a grieving husband, who mourned the fact that the early promise of a happy marriage had not been fulfilled, and who could never understand that the fault had not been all on her side. He spent long hours in prayer in front of the marble shrine in which her heart had been enclosed and perhaps came nearer to her in death than he had ever been during her life. Her two sons were desolate, but facets of her personality lived on in each of them. Charles inherited her charm and unpredictable personality and Henry her devotion to religion.

Her death cast a deep gloom over the Muti Palace but it was not to cause the Nithsdales as much pain as what was to befall them a few months later. Lord Bellew had decided to return to England with Anne and their three-year-old daughter Frances. Anne was expecting her second child, but as Mrs Lindsay was to travel with her and be with her at the birth, her parents had no fears when they wished them goodbye. In fact it was hoped that Lord Bellew's affairs could be better settled in England and that they could look forward to a more comfortable life there.

They first took lodgings in London where Anne gave birth to a little boy, Edward. After the birth she became ill and began to suffer from a fever. Her husband and his relatives made every effort to find the best physicians possible and Mrs Lindsay never left her bedside. When it was suggested that a "nurse-keeper" should come to look after the patient, Mrs Lindsay insisted that she was perfectly well able to discharge the doctor's orders and Anne was happier being looked after by her life-long companion and nurse. When the illness took a turn for the worse, Mrs Lindsay, without consulting anyone, decided that the medicines that had been prescribed were making Anne suffer and she ceased to adminster them to her. Within a few days, to the misery of all around her, Anne was dead.

Lord Bellew was heart-broken and when he discovered that Mrs Lindsay had not been giving his wife the medicines that the doctors had prescribed, he could not help blaming her for Anne's death. The unfortunate woman, who had cared for Anne with single-minded devotion since Anne was four and had hoped to spend the rest of her life with her, was inconsolable.

The news of Anne's death was a cruel blow for the Nithsdales, who had rejoiced in the fact that she had been happily married. In her grief, Winifred felt she was in some way responsible, and wrote shortly afterwards to John Bellew, ". . . my daughter whom God Almighty having been pleased to take from me in punishment of my sins."

The baby, Edward, in spite of all the care lavished on him, survived only a few months, but Frances was a robust little girl. By the terms of the marriage contract the Nithsdales were to be responsible for her upbringing. Lord Bellew arranged for the child to be escorted back to Rome by Mrs Lindsay and promised to send an allowance for her maintenance and was adamant that if Winifred or her husband became ill or were unable to continue to look after her, he would take her back to live with him.

Any apprehension that the Nithsdales might have felt about caring for their small granddaughter was soon dispelled. They doted on the little girl, who was a living reminder of Anne, and they lavished on her the care and affection that they had been unable to give to their own children.

At first Lord Bellew wrote regularly to find out how his daughter was getting on and promised to let them know when he had sorted out his affairs. Then nothing more was heard from him for another four years. When Frances was seven years old, Winifred learnt from mutual friends that Lord Bellew had remarried. His second wife was an Irish lady, the wealthy widow of the Earl of Fingal, and they now had a baby daughter. He had never informed his former parents-in-law of this event and Winifred had to write him a strong letter reminding him that Frances had so far "not cost him a penny" but she was now in need of masters and what was he prepared to do about it? She was also naturally worried about the child's future and wanted him to put some money in trust for her.

It took eighteen months for Winifred to receive a reply but when the letter arrived its contents were very satisfactory. Lord Bellew made the excuse that his previous letter must have gone astray and he put forward the financial provision he intended to make for his daughter. He would settle five thousand on her and more if he should die without a male heir. He would provide a £100 a year for her maintenance which would be remitted to Lady Nithsdale quarterly and he was sending immediately eight hundred crowns to cover her past expenses if this was agreeable. He said that he had heard that little Frances was very like her mother, and that he longed to have more news of her, and asked if she could write him a short note in "her own natural style".

These generous promises were not all fulfilled and William had become so devoted to his granddaughter that he even put pen to paper himself, and got in touch Lord Bellew's bishop in Ireland. The bishop acted as a negotiator and informed him that Lord Bellew had "several law suits and troubles" as his second wife had died recently but he had every intention of supporting his daughter. These aspirations were finally fulfilled and the Nithsdales no long had to worry about the future of their granddaughter. Later that year, in gratitude for his long and loyal service, James granted Lord Nithsdale the Order of the Thistle. William responded by immediately sending off to Paris for a green silk ribbon to put it on.

Meanwhile a resurgence of Jacobite loyalty and a strong desire for a Stuart restoration had passed to the next generation. Lord Derwentwater's younger brother, Charles Radcliffe, had escaped from Newgate prison and he and his wife had come to live in Rome. Their house had become a meeting place for young Jacobites and many a young gentleman on the grand tour found his views turned by this charismatic couple. Stosch complained that this "furious and headstrong enthusiast" be removed but it was he himself who finally retreated to Florence, leaving the British consul in Rome "the only person in all Italy that the British government could rely upon".

The British government still looked on the Jacobite menace seriously. Though they could safely say that they had written off "old Mr Melancholy" as they now referred to James, they could not ignore his two sons. As Walpole wrote to Mann, his minster in Florence: "We despise the court of Rome in England very justly in one respect but too much in another. One should consider what weight its opinions have all over Italy and in most parts of Europe. . . ."

Prince Charles Edward Stuart (circle of Louis Tocque).

CHAPTER 30

Prince Charles leaves for Scotland

Since royal Prince Charles is come to this land,
To fight for his country, his sword in his hand;
He's put on his plaid, and also his trouze
To honour the Scots, give the English their dues

The Nithsdales watched with pride as the two princes grew into good-looking young men who commanded attention wherever they went. When they appeared at balls adorned in their Sobieski jewels they were the epitome of everything a young prince should be. Charles, lean and fair with brown eyes and a sensuous mouth was much admired for his perfect manners and engaging personality, while Winifred's erstwhile charge, the little duke, was more stockily built and with his dark colouring and even features was generally considered to be the more handsome of the two. Though equally fond of sport and dancing, he had a more serious nature and for a time during his adolescence, became so religious that it verged on obsession. Both young men were also accomplished musicians; Charles played the cello and Henry had a good voice. James adored both his sons, even to their detriment, and it was observed that Charles was inclined to be headstrong.

Visitors from England were curious to get a glimpse of the two princes and rumours were circulating that Charles was to become engaged to the French Princess. Lady Wortley Montagu gazed at them curiously when she saw them at a public ball. She was surprised by the richness of their dress and seeming affluence. The eldest she described as "careless enough" while the youngest "danced finely and had an ingenuous countenance." The poet, Gray, could find nothing ill to say about the princes but described the unfortunate James as having an "uncompromising countenance and the look of an idiot, particularly when he laughs or prays". He reported that he lived very privately with his little court about him consisting of "Lord Dunbar who manages everything and two or three Preston Lords who would be very glad to make their peace at home".

At the age of fourteen, Charles had already shown courage when he had cut his teeth in battle with the Spanish army at the Seige of Gaeta, and had subsequently toured Europe, where he had been treated everywhere as a king-to-be. The time was ripe for him to take up his father's cause, and he was only too eager to listen to the envoys who arrived in Rome voicing the enthusiasm of the new generation of leaders in Britain. Several recent events had taken place which had given a new lease of life to the Jacobite cause. In England their old enemy, Sir Robert Walpole, had left the Commons and had taken himself off to the House of Lords. In France, Louis XV had suffered a humiliating defeat by the British at the battle of Dettingen and was only too eager to take his revenge. The peace-loving Cardinal Fleury had died and had been succeeded by Cardinal de Tencin, one of James's old friends. While in Rome the new Pope, Benedict XIV, was showing a particular interest in getting the Stuarts back on the British throne, though their antagonists maintained that this was only because he was anxious to get them out of the Holy City.

In Scotland, the Earl of Traquair had died and Charles Linton had succeeded to the title. He and his brother John Stuart, had espoused the Jacobite cause with fervour. They had joined an association of Jacobite leaders called "The Concert" which had the aim of bringing the Highland and Lowland nobles together and had also signed the Scotch Bond to encourage Jacobites to lend money for a rebellion. When the disunity of the Jacobites in England made Scotland the most likely place for the prince to land, Traquair and John Stuart had already, with other leaders, signed a letter to Cardinal Fleury listing the exact number of arms men and the amount of money that would be needed to overcome the government troops and they had pledged their support if these could be provided.

After long negotiations between the Jacobites in Scotland, France and England, it was decided that, as the English would not commit themselves in writing, the Rising should be started in Scotland, and Louis was finally persuaded to prepare vessels with the needed supplies.

By January 14th 1744, all was ready and Charles was asked to come to France. He left Rome secretly, the truth even being hidden from his younger brother, Henry, who was told that he had only gone into the country to hunt boar. Henry was so fond of his brother that it was feared that had he known the truth he would have been unable to hide his anxiety. James, who had lost his ambition since the accession of George II, was loath to see him go. To his son's dramatic farewell, "I go sire in the search of three crowns which I doubt not to have the honour and happiness to lay at your Majesty's feet," he answered sadly, "Heaven forbid that all the crowns of the world shall rob me of my son". He may well have had a premonition of the outcome for though James was to live another twenty years, he was never to see his son again.

Winifred's concerns at this time were only for her husband who had fallen ill and who died a few months before Prince Charles's departure. Her love for William had allowed her to overcome her exasperation at his perpetual profligacy but it was only after his death that she became fully aware of the extent of the money that was owed. The creditors began to close in on her and with the help of Lord Dunbar (Murray), who had become a kind friend, she wrote in desperation to her son for help. His own finances

Charles, Lord Linton, later 5th Earl of Traquair (Amigoni).

were still not on a strong footing and he now had other matters on his mind. He was slow in replying, and her anxiety over her obligations, combined with the grief for the loss of her husband of forty-four years, broke her spirit and she became ill. The rector of the Scots College in Rome took pity on her and negotiated with William to send his mother enough money to settle the debts over three years. It was not long before Winifred recovered her health and, with great economy, she managed to pay them off in one year.

In March 1744, Prince Charles boarded one of the well armed fleet of French ships, bearing all the supplies that had been asked for, and under the command of Marshal Saxe, prepared to set sail for Scotland. Yet once more their old adversary, the sea, dashed the Stuart's hopes. As the French fleet prepared to set sail for Scotland a savage storm blew up causing havoc among the fleet and several ships were lost. Immediatley afterwards the British, whose spies had discovered the details of the proposed landing, were seen appearing in the Channel. Louis had a change of heart and decided to postpone the expedition. Bored and frustrated, Charles lingered on in France while Louis kept him in suspense.

Lady Carrington and her niece had returned to Paris and while he was waiting Charles went to visit her. Now eighty-five, this intrepid woman had arrived back from Spain with her niece, complete with mineral rights to "one of the riches mines in Europe" and was attempting to raise enough money to work it. She was optimistically hoping to accomplish this by the end of the year and her great fortune, she assured Winifred, would make them all "easy". She found the prince "very gracious and affable" and he spoke of Winifred "with a great deal of esteem".

After months of indecision, Charles heard that France had decided to postpone the landing in Scotland indefinitely. Bitterly disappointed and unable to get any further promise of commitment from the French, he made up his mind against all advice that he would go whatever, "even though with a single footman".

When the Jacobites in Scotland heard this foolhardy intention they were thrown into confusion. The members of the Buck Club, a Jacobite club founded by Murray of Broughton which met regularly in Edinburgh, were divided in their views. Some of the members still insisted that they would support the Prince however he came but others, (including Lord Traquair) were more cautious and in favour of imposing conditions. Finally a vote was taken and the majority decided that, unless the Prince could bring 6000 regular troops, arms for 10,000 more, and 30,000 louis d'or, he should not come as the expedition would be bound to fail. A letter was written to this effect, and Charles Traquair was commissioned to take it to London, and find a messenger to deliver it to the prince in France. The Earl, however, had more important matters on his mind. He was bent on wooing an heiress, Teresa Conyers, and on his way south he went to visit her. He returned four months later with the letter still in his pocket and excused himself by saying that he had been unable to find a courier. Although another messenger was immediately dispatched it was too late. Prince Charles had already left Paris.

He had borrowed as much money as he was able and had hired two vessels. He fitted them out himself and spent every penny he had on arms and ammunition. In June he set sail for Scotland. Again misfortune overtook him. The largest ship, *L'Elizabeth* with 700 men and a good supply of arms, was damaged, and was forced to return to France. The prince decided to continue and finally landed with only seven supporters and 4000 louis d'or.

The story of the prince's success in winning over the Highlanders is well known but once again the Jacobites in the Lowlands had to make up their minds what action to take. William Maxwell wavered till the last minute. On 13th October 1745, after the Battle of Prestonpans, he wrote to an acquaintance, "I am determined to take a share in the present enterprise ... only be assured I'll do nothing rashly, that's only for desperados". When the prince reached Edinburgh on his march south, William, together with Lord Kenmure, was summoned to dine at the Castle. Both men, whose fathers had suffered in the 1715 Rebellion, were asked to join the prince's army. They requested to be allowed to return home to consider their answers. After a short interval both sent their excuses. As the prince's army marched through anti-Jacobite Dumfries where they were not well received, William was obliged to go into hiding and his terrifed wife Catherine asked her mother to allow her to take refuge at Traquair.

In the event, neither of William's cousins "came out". John Stuart's young wife, Christina Anstruther, implored her mother-in-law to dissuade her son from taking part in the "public enterprise" while Charles occupied himself in successfully gaining Teresa Conyer's hand and marrying her. When he was picked up after the Rebellion and incarcerated in the Tower of London she volunteered to share his imprisonment.

Winifred died peacefully in Rome in 1749, two years after Prince Henry was made a cardinal.

Bear Gates, Traquair House, by legend closed in 1745 and not to be reopened until there is a Stuart king on the throne. Photograph: Scottish Tourist Board.

Appendix I

Some years after Lady Nithsdale had rescued her husband from the Tower of London, her sister, Lucy Herbert, Prioress of the English Convent in Bruges, asked her to write an account of the escape. The letter is still kept in the Convent archives.

Undated.

Deare Sister,

My Lord's escape is such an old story now, that I have almost forgott it, but since you desire the account, to whom I have too many obligations to refuse anything that is in my power, I will endeavour to call it to mind, and be as exact in the relations as possible. I think I owe my selfe the justice to begin by the motives I had to atempt so hazardous an enterprise, which I fully intended not to goe about till the very last, forseeing all the dificultys, which could not be surmounted without a perticular protection of almighty God, but rely'd it would not be refused me, when all human resources fail'd. You must then know, that when I first came to London, which I did as soon as ever I heard of my Lord's being in the Tower, and he earnest desire I should, he, as he sent me word, having noe body to help him till I came, upon which I rode to Newcastle, and took the coach there to York, but there fell so much snow, that when I came thither, the York coach could not goe, so I took horses and rode to London. Through such weather, the very post stopt some dayes, and we were up to the horse girts in the snow; however, I gott safe and without accident. When arrived, I went immediately and solicited all the persons in power, without the least hopes given me of any favour; all the contrary, every one was so plain as to tell me that perhaps some of the prisoners might be pardon'd, but not him for certain. I beg'd to know the occasion of this distinction, but could obtain noe answer to that point, but that they would not flater me, which tho' they did not tell me, well did I know the reasons: A Catholic upon the Borders, and one who had a great following, and whos family had ever upon all occasions stuck to the royal family, and the only suport the Catholicks had amongst that Whigish part of the countrey, would be well out of the way. They had not yet forgot that his grandfather held out, as the last garison in Scotland, his own Castle of Carlaverock, and rendered it up by the King's own orders, so that, now they had him in their power, they were resolved not to let him slip out of their hands. Upon which I took the resolution to endeavour his escape, but confided my intention to noe body me dear Evans. But to concert measures, I solicited earnestly to be permited to see my Lord, but that was refused me, except I would stay in prison with him; that I would not accept, giving for reason that my health would not agree with such a confinement: but the true one was, that I would than put my selfe out of the power of doing what I intended to atempt. But by meanes of money to the guards I saw him frequently, till the condemnation, after which we had leave, the last week, to go and take our leaves of them. I had provided all that was necessary for his disguise, by meanes of poor Evans, so had nothing to doe but persuad him to make use of them, which I had much difficulty to doe. However God Almighty help me in that also when the time came. It was on a Thursday, 22nd February, that our general petition to the House of Lords was given, to beg them to interseed to the king to pardon the prisoners, having been , having been disapointed the day before of its being deliver'd, because the Duke ———-, I forgot which of the bastard Dukes, had promised Lady Darwentwater to give it, and when it came to, he fail'd, and as she was an English Countess, it was her business. However, we had still the next day before the execution, in which he promised not to faile. But for feare he should, I ingaged the Duke of Montrose, so I was sure of its being done by one or the other, and therefore went with a most numerous train of most of the ladys of quality then in town, to solicit their favour as the Lords went into the Parliament House, who all treated me very civilly. But the favour we gott was cheefly due to poor Lord Pembrok, who though he beg'd me not to come near him, sent me word he would doe all that Lay in his power which he perform'd fully, for it was upon a speech of his that it pased in our favours. The occasion of the petition was, that they pretended to dispute the King's power of pardoning prisoners Parliament had accused. Butä by the forementiond person's speech it was caryed that it was, and they granted our petition to them to interseed to him for mercy; but there rose up one of the Lords, and said they would doe so, but with this clause, that should be for such of them that "deserved it", and not in general. This took of all my hopes, for I understood that these deserts consisted in informations of all those that were engaged in the business; and well did I know, nor wouldä I have desired, that my Lord should have purchased his life at that rate; however, the grantä in general I thought I might make a benefit of my design, and with this thought, went strait out of the Parliament House to the Tower, and putting on as cheerful a look as I was able, went up, and told the guards at each place where they were, that I came to bring good newse about their prisoners, for there was now noe fear of them, the petition having pass'd in their favour, and then pull'd out some small thing out of my poket, and bid them drink the King's health, and the Peers. What I gave them was noe great matter, for I was affraid that if I gave them too liberaly they might perhaps thinke I had some design, and I thought giving of them somthing would put them in good humour against the next day, which was the last before that appointed for the execution. The morning after I did not goe, (but in the afternoon,) having too many things to put in readiness. When I was ready to goe, I sent to Mrs. Mills, in whos house I was lodg'd, and told her that, finding there was now noe further room for hope of my Lord's pardon, nor longer time but this night, I was resolved to indeavour his escape; that I had provided all that was requisit for it, and that I hop't she would not refuse to come allong with me, to the end that he might pass for her, and beg'd she could come imediately, because we were full late. In the meane while, I sent to one Mrs Morgan, who than went by the name of Hilton, one my dear Evans had made me aquainted with, who had render'd me a great service. She I also told my intention to, and desired, she being tall and slender, she would put under her own riding hood one I had provided to put upon Mrs Mills, who was to give hers to my Lord, my intention being that when he came out he should pass for her; she was as tall as him, and being with child, would be about the same bigness. After which we went into the coach, where I never ceased talking, not to give them leasure to think, for they consented imediatley to come with me, the surprise having left them noe time to reflect of the consequences. When we arrived, the first I brought in was Mrs. Morgan, for I could cary in but one at once, and she brought in the cloaths that was to serve Mrs. Mills when she had parted with her own; and after I had stript her of what she had brought in for me; I conducted her out again, beging she would doe me the kindness to send me my woman to drease me, for I began to be affraid I should be too late if she did not come imediately, having a petition to give, which if I were too late, having but this night, I were undone, so dispatch'd her safe, and partly down stairs, where I took Mrs. Mills who came in with her handkerchief before her eyes, as it was very natural for a person that came to take leave of a freind that was going to die. I made her doe it, that he might go out in the same manner; and her eyebrows being a little upon the yalow, and his very thick and black, I had provided paint of that colour to dy his, and a tour of the same collour'd hair, and paint to comer it with, and the rest of his face, and red for the cheeks, all which remainder of the provission I left in the Tower when I went out. The poor guards, who upon the little I had given them the night before, were in good humour lett me in and out with my people very willingly, and were not so much upon the qui vivre, because they were persuaded there would be a pardon, upon what I had told them the day before. I made Mrs Mills put of her own rideing hood, and put on that I had brought in, which, when she had done, I took her by the hand and went out with her of my Lord's room, saying as I pass'd through the other (in which there were 9 people), with all the seeming concern imagineable - Dear Mrs. Cathrin, I must beg you to goe in all heast and look for my woman, for she certinaly does not know what a clock it is, and has forgott the pitition I am to give, which, should I miss, is irrepairable, having but this one night; lett her make all the heast she can possible, for I shall be upon thorns till she comes. So the person in the room, who were all the guards' wives and daughters, seem'd all to be in pain, and the sentinells at the door opeen'd it very speedily, and when I had seen out I return'd to my Lord, and made an end of putting him in order. I had taken care that Mrs. Mills, when she went out should not goe crying as I had made her come in, because my Lord might pass for the gentlewoman that came in so, having her cloths, which when I had finished to put him on, with all my petticoats but one, it grew prety dark, and I was affraid of the lighting of the candles, so thought it was time to goe, so I came out, leading hem by the hand, he had his handkerchief before his eyes, and I spoak to him with the greatest concern in the world, lamenting my selfe bitterly that Evans was so neglectful, that she had ruine'd me by her long stay, so, dear Mrs Betty, run and bring her with you for God sake; you know my lodgings, and if ever you made heast in your life doe it now, for I am almost distracted by this disapointment. So the guard oppen'd the door very quickly, and I went with him downstairs, still conjuring him to make heast; but as soon as I gott him out of the door, I made him passe before, and I followed him for feare the sentinell had preceaved som thing by his way of walking, but I still continued to beg him to make heast. At the foot of the staires I found my dear Evan, in whos hands I put him. I had engaged Mr Mills to expect in the place before the Tower, to carry him to some sure place in case we succeeded. But he thought it so improbable that we should, that the surprise at the sight made him loose him selfe so intirely that he was capble of nothing which my dear Evans perceiving, and having all the presence of mind imagineable, and having friends of her she could confide, she imediately, without telling him any thing for feare it should strick him, caryed him to a place of security, or else we had lost our business after it was done: And having left him there, return'd to look for Mr Mills who by this time was come from his surprise and gone home, and had procured a place for him to stay in, which they cary'd him to. In the meanwhile, I who had sent him as it were of a mesuage, was obliged to return upstairs and pass the room again to goe to my Lord's in the same seeming perplexity for fear of being to late as I went down in, so that all the poor people seem'd to compassionat me mightely. When I gott into my Lord's chamber, I spoak to him as it were, and I answer'd as if he had, and imitated his voice as near as I could, and walk'd up and down the room, as if we had been walking and talking together, till I though he had time enough to be out of their reach. I than begun to thinke it was fitt for me to gett out of it also. So I oppen'd the door, and went halfe out of it, holding the door in my hand, that what I said might be heard by those without, and took a solemn leave of my Lord for that night, saying that I thought some starnge thing must have hapen'd to make Evans stay, she that never used to be neglectfull in the smalest thing, to make her so in a matter of this concequence. But I found there was noe remedy but going my selfe; that if the Tower was still oppen when I had done, I would see him that night, but he might be sure that as soon as ever it was in the morning, I would be with him, and hoped to bring him good newse, and then before I shutt the door, I drew in to the inside a little string that lifted up a wooden latche, so that when the string was wantingä in the outside, the door could not be oppen'd but by those within, after which I shut the door with a flap, that it might be surely shut, and as I pass'd by I told my Lord's valet de chamber, who knew nothing of the matter, that he would not have candles till he call'd for them, for that he would finish some prayers first, and so went down stairs. And there being several hackeney coaches waiting in the place, I gott into one and went to my own lodging, whereä I had left poor Mr Makenzy to stay for the petition that was to have been given in case my project had fail'd, for it was not come before I went. So I told him there was noe need of it now, for my Lord was out of the Tower and their hands, I hopet, but as yett did not know where. I disharg'd the coach I had taken at the Tower, and made them call me a chair, and went ot the Dutchess of Boclugh who was staying at home for me, for I had engaged her to come along with me to give it, because I had been so used in the last. I ask't if she were at home, and who was with her; they told me she was, and stay'd for me, and that she had some Dutchess with her, but I forgot who. I said since she had company I would not goe up, being very unfitt for any, but beg'd the favour of some room to stay in below till they would doe me the kindness to call my Lady's woman to me, for I had a word to say to her. I had discharged the chair when I cam in for feare of being persued. When the gentlewoman came down I desired she would present my most humble service to her Grace, whom I heard had company, and therefore did not care to goe up my selfe, and tell he that I was very much obig'd to her for the favour she had promis'd me, of going with me to give my petition, but that she need not give her selfe any further trouble, it being now thought fitt to give a general petition in the name of us all. So I would not give a perticular one, but that I would not forget my obligation to her, and would take my time of coming to thank her for it my selfe. After which I made one of the servants call me a chair, and bid them goe to the Dutchess of Montrose, who had all along shew'd perticular concern for me. She had left word that in case I came, to say she was not at home, because the said she could not see me in the trouble she knew I would be in, but by some mistake they brought me up, there was noe remedy. So she came to me, and as my heart was very light, I smil'd when she came into the chamber, and run to her in great joy. She realy started when she saw me, and since own'd that she thought my head was turn'd with trouble, till I told her my good fortune; after which she beg'd meä to put my selfe in place of security, for that she knew the Electour was highly displeased with me for the petition I had given him that had occasion'd his being complained of. I desired they would call me a chair, for I never kept any for feare of being tris'd. The Dutchess said she would goe to Court and see how the newse was receiv'd, which she did, and told me the Electour storm'd terribly when the account came, and said he was betray'd, for he was sureä it could not have been done without connivance, and sent two persons to the Tower imediately to see that the others were well guarded, that they might not doe the like. Some said it was one, the other another, and noe body was very sure which, but herselfe. After I left her, I went to a house which Evans had found for me before hand, where she had promis'd to come and give me notice where my Lord was, which she did soon after I was there, and told me that, after she had left him in security, she went to seek out Mr Mills who by that time was come from his first surprise and return'd to his own house, where she found him, and that he cary'd my Lord from the first place where she put him in the mean whileä to a poor woman's house just before the court of guards. She had but one litle room up a small pair of stairs, a poor litle bed, into which were were forced to goe imedeately for feare they shouold heare more walking than usual. She left us a botle of wine and some bread, and Mrs. Mills brought us some more the next day in her poket, but other thing we gott not from Thursday evening to Saturday evening, that Mr Mills came when it was dark, and cary'd my Lord to the Venetian Embacedor's who knew nothing of the matter. But one of the servants kept him in his own room til Wensday, he being to goe to Dover by the Ebacedor's orders, with a coach and six horse, to bring his brother from thence; whom he expected by that time. He put my Lord on a livery coat, and went over to Calis with my Lord in so few hours that the master of it said, if we were flying for our lives we could not have a fairer wind, which he said by chance, litle thinking that he had one in it that was in that case. Mr Michell might have return'd back without being suspected to have had a hand in it, but my Lord, I supose, had an inclination he should goe allong with him, which he did, and is now very well placed with our young master. This is as full account as I can give you of that affair, and all those concern'd in it, and I assure you is as near as I can possibly remember just as it past, and you may depend upon the truth. For my part, I went into a very honest man's house in Drury Laine, but whos name I doe not remember, and lay quiet till I heard my Lord was safe of the other side of the watter; and than I wrote a letter to the Dutchess of Boclugh (till which time it was thought I was gone with my Lord, so I was not searched for,) in which I told her that I heard that I was suspected to have procured my Lord's escape; that realy it was so naturaly to be believed if I had been so happy as to have had it in my power; that I did not blame them for thinking it, but their suspission, without prouf, was not sufficient to make me suffer for a suposed crime, but enough to occasion my being secured, so beg'd she would be pleased to obtain me leave to goe with safety about my business. Insteed of obtaining, they were resolved to indeavour to find me out, but after several debates about it, Mr Solicitour-General, (a man I had never seen nor knew anything of,) said, since I had so much deference for the Government as not to appear, it would be a cruelty to search for me. So, upon his speach it was resolved that, in case I kept out of the way, noe particular search would be made for me, but if I appear'd in either of the 2 kingdoms, England or Scotland, I should be imediately secured. But that favour was not sufficient for me, except I left my sone a beggar, for my Lord sending for me in such heast, I had time for nothing; and having all the family papers in my hands, and noe body fitt to be trusted with them, my house lyable to be search'd when ever they pleas'd, and concequently noe security for them, I took the resolution, as the only thing I could than doe, to bury them, and noe body but my selfe and the gardener knew where they were, or any thing of the matter; and it was well I did it, for the house was often search'd after I went of. And God knows what account had been had of them. This madeä my presence of absolute necessity, or they had been ruin'd; for though, with much care, they had laine safe one very hard winter without suffering, (for when I took them up they wereä as dry as if they had been by the fire side,) it was not possible they could have laine without prejudice, so, as I had riskt my life for the father, I was resolved to run a second risk for the benefit of the son, tho' I had never rid but the foremention'd journey from York, but now ill weather was not the case, but feare of being known, and by consequence ceased, which to avoid, I bought 3 sadle horses, and went down a horse back, accompany'd only by my deare Evans, and a very trusty man I brought with me out of Scotland. We lodg'd in all the small inns that was capable of receibving a few horses, where I was sure not to be known, for inä all the best I was so, on both roads. By this meanes I gott safe to Traquire. There I was safe, for the leuetenant of the county, being my Lord's friend, would not search for me without giving privat notice, that I might gett out of the way. So there I venter'd to rest my selfe two dayes, seeming to have noe feare upon me, but made it pass as if I was come to goe home with leave of the Government, but sent noe notice to my own house, because I would not give the Magistrats of Dumfrise time to inquire about me. So they knew nothing of my arrival in the countrey, till I came home, where I made it pass as if I had leave to doe it, and to convince them the better, sent to all my neighbours about my being come, and that I long'd to see them; in the mean while I lifted my papers by night, and sent them imediately to Traquire, which was a providence I made such heast to doe, for they were not long before they began to suspect me; and some persons happen'd to heare the Magistraits say, that they were resolved to goe the next day, and wit upon me, and see the leave I had from the Government. This was told me by way of newse, which, when I heard, I reply'd, I must confess I am a little surprised they have been so long a coming; now I have been here 3 dayes, and they have not yet pay'd their duty to me, but it is better late than never, pray tell them they shall be very wellcom when they please. This was in the afternoon, but I staidä not a minut without ordering all things to be gott ready very privately, and the next morning, by break of day, I went of with the same company, and gott safe to London, lodging as before in the by inns. When I arrived, I found they still discourced of my having been in Scotland, notwithstanding the prohibision; and one of the ladys told me that the Electour was highly displeased when he heard it, gave orders for my being searched for; that I did whatä I pleased in spight of his heart, and the I had done him more mischeif than any woman in Christendom; so I lay quiet till the hubub and search was over. In the mean while I took the advice of a very honest and famous lawyer, who was of opinion that it was fit for me to be gone, after the search for me was over; which advice I follow'd about a fortnight later, and gott safe without accident. The reason he gave me for it was, that tho' in all other cases a wife could not be persued for making her husband's escape, but in the matter of treason, according to the rigour of the law, a wife's head answers for her husband's and the Electour was so enraged at me, that they would not answer what might happen; so beg'd me to be gone. The reason of this great displeasure had been augmented by a petition I had given him, notwithstanding his orders that noe body should offer to come with any of the prisoner's wives to give him any, for he was resolved not to be troubled with any. But my Lord had a great inclination to have a pitition given thinking it might be of benefit; for my part, I did not think it would be of any, but was willing to content him, so desir'd him to have his pitition drawn, and I would find a way to deliver it, notwithstanding all the precaution the Elctour had taken to avoid it; so the first day that I knew he was to goe to the drawing room, I dressed my selfe in a black mantow and peticoat, as if in mourning, and sent to Mrs Morgan, the same as went with me to the Tower afterwards, as before mention'd, for I did not know the Electour, and might have taken another for him, and she did, so would show me the right. I had another gentlewoman with me, but I forgot who, but we went all 3 into the chamber that was between his closet and the drawing room, so that he was to pass the whole length of the room to goe to it, and there being three window in it, we sat our selves upon the midle one, that I might have time to catche him before he could get by, which I did, and knelt down and presented my petition, telling him in French that I was the unhappy Countess of Nithsdaill, that he might not pretend he knew not who I was, but finding him going without taking my petition, I took hold of the skirt of his coat, that he might stay to heare me; but he indeavour'd to get away, and I held so fast, that he drew me upon my knees almost from the midle of the chamber to the drawing room door;' at last one of the Bleu Ribonds that was with him took me round the waist to draw me back, and another drew the skirt of his coat out of my hand and the petition that I had indeavour'd to put in his poket fell down in the strugle, and I almost swounded with the trouble; how ever, one of the gentlemen took up the petition, and as I knew it ought to have been given by him to the Lord of the Bed Chamber that was in waiting, I had write a letter before hand, and desired he would doe me the favour to have a petition read that I had had the honour to give to the King, as I was forced to term him. It proved to be my Lord Docet, by good luck for me, it was one Mrs. Morgan was very well acquainted with, she went into the drawing room, and deliver'd the letter to him, which he took very civilly, but could not than read it, for he was at cards with the Prince, but as soon as the game was ended, he did, and acted, as I heard, very warmly and kindly in the matter, to which he was induced the more by the Duke of Montrose who had seen me as he had pass'd into the room, and was than coming to speak to me, but I made him a sign not to doe it, for feare his takening notice of me might have spoilt my design. They gott my petition to be read more than once, without any effect, but served for the discource there that night, and my being so rudely treated had made a noise, and gave no good reputation to the Duke of Hanover, for several said, what had they brought themselves to, for the Kings of England was never used to refuse a petition from the poorest woman's hand, and to use a person of my quality in such a manner as he had done, was a piece of unheard of brutality; these talkes made the Elector have a perticular dislike to me, which he shew'd afterward, for when all the ladys whos lords had been concern'd in this business, put in clames for their jointures, mine was given amongs the rest, but he said I was not, nor did deserve the same privilege; so I was excepted, and he would never heare speak in my favour. This made every one of opinion I was better out of the way, for in the fury they were then against me, it was not adviseable for me to venter into their hands; upon which I went of. This is the full relation of what you desired, and of all the transactions that I pass'd at that time, which noe body but your selfe could have obtained from me, for whom my obligations has imposed me a law of never refusin any that lys in my power. You will excuse all mistakes in this long scroll, for it being only to you, I rely'd on your goodness in that, and have had noe other regard but to the truth, that you may depend upon; and all other faults you must excuse.

Appendix 2

FAMILY TREE SHOWING CONNECTION BETWEEN WINIFRED HERBERT AND WILLIAM MAXWELL (LORD NITHSDALE)

LADY LUCY DOUGLAS — m — ROBERT MAXWELL 4th Earl of Nithsdale

WILLIAM HERBERT 3rd Lord Powis 1st Earl 1st Marquis created 1st Duke by JAMES II in exile — m — LADY ELIZABETH SOMERSET

Children of William Herbert and Lady Elizabeth Somerset:

- MARY m SIR GEORGE MAXWELL
- FRANCES m LORD SEAFORTH
- ANNE m VISCOUNT CARRINGTON
- WILLIAM HERBERT 2nd Marquis of Powis
- LUCY Prioress English Convent Bruges
- WINIFRED HERBERT

Children of Lady Lucy Douglas and Robert Maxwell:

- MARY MAXWELL
- WILLIAM MAXWELL 5th Earl of Nithsdale

CHARLES STUART 4th Earl of Traquair — m — MARY MAXWELL

WILLIAM MAXWELL 5th Earl of Nithsdale — m — WINIFRED HERBERT

Children of Charles Stuart and Mary Maxwell: 17 children including

- CHARLES LORD LINTON 5th Earl of Traquair m TERESA CONYERS
- JOHN STUART m CHRISTINA ANSRUTHER
- LUCY STUART
- ANNE STUART
- MARY STUART
- CATHERINE STUART

Children of William Maxwell and Winifred Herbert:

- WILLIAM MAXWELL (Nithsdale title attained after 1715)
- ANNE MAXWELL m JOHN LORD BELLEW

CATHERINE STUART — m — WILLIAM MAXWELL

Children of Catherine Stuart and William Maxwell:

- MARY MAXWELL
- WINIFRED MAXWELL

Appendix 3

TABLE OF THE 57 PERSONS WITH A BETTER CLAIM TO THE THRONE OF GREAT BRITAIN IN 1714 THAN THE ELECTRESS SOPHIA AND HER SON GEORGE LEWIS (GEORGE I)

- JAMES I of England, Scotland and Ireland
  - Charles I
    - Charles II
    - James II
    - Henriette Anne, m. Philip of Orleans. 3 children
      - Philip o.s.p.
      - Marie L., o.s.p., Queen of Spain
      - Anne Marie, 2nd heir, m. Victor Amadeus I, of Savoy
        - 3. Philip, Prince of Piedmont, o.s.p.
        - 4. Charles, Duke of Aosta, b. 1701 (afterwards Charles Emmanuel III, King of Sardinia.
        - Marie Adelaide, m. Duke of Burgundy.
          - 5. Dauphin, afterwards Louis XV
        - Marie Gabrielle, m. Philip V of Spain. 3 sons
          - 6. Louis, King of Spain
          - 7. Philip
          - 8. Ferdinand VI, King of Spain, o.s.p.
  - Elizabeth, Queen of Bohemia
    - Charles Lewis, Elector Palatine
      - 9. (Charlotte Elizabeth) second wife of Philip, Duke of Orleans
        - 10. Philip, Regent of Orleans. 1 son, 5 dau.
          - 11. Louis, Duke of Chartres.
          - 12. Duchess of Berry
          - 13. Mad. d' Orleans
          - 14. Mad. d' Valois
          - 15. Mad. d' Montpensier
          - 16. Mad. de Beaujolais, b. 1714
        - 17. Eliz., Duchess of Lorraine. 3 sons , 2 dau.
          - 18. Leopold
          - 19. Francis
          - 20. Charles
          - 21. Elizabeth
          - 22. Anne Charlotte

The descendants of all of these, and of others born after 1716 in the same families, now number many hundreds

After the 2 daughters of the Emperor Joseph I, came the Electress Sophia, and her son as 58 and 59. The Electress died in June 1714, only seven weeks before Queen Anne, aged 86. Her husband was Ernest Augustus, younger brother of Fredric, Duke of Brunswick-Luneberg-Hanover, and he eventually became Elector of Hanover

Edward, Count Palatine, became an R.C.

Marie Pr. of Salmes. 1 son, 2 dau

23. Louis Otto. 3 dau.

24. Dorothea
25. Elizabeth
26. Christine

27. Adelaide
28. Eleonore

29. Anne, Princess of Conti

Louis, Duc de Bourbon. 3 sons, 6 dau.

30. Louis de Bourbon
31. Charles de Charolais
32. Mlle. de Clermont
33. Maria-Anne de Bourbon
34. Louis de Conti
35. Mad. de Charolais
36. Mad. de Clermont
37. Mad. de Vermandois
38. Mad. de Sens

39. Marie de Conti 1 son, 2 dau.

40. Louis, Prince of Conti
41. Marie, Duch of Bourbon
42. Louis de Conti

43. Louise, D. de Maine. 2 sons, 1 dau.

44. Louis
45. Louis Ch.
46. Mad. de Maine

47. Marie, 3rd dau. of Anne de Conti

48. Benedicte, m. Frederick, Duke of Brunswick-Luneberg. 2 dau

49. Charlotte, m. Renaud of Modena. 2 sons, 3 dau..

50. Francis of Modena
51. Frederic
52. Benedicte
53. Amelia Josephea
54. Henrietta
*

55. Wilhelmina m. Jos. I (1705-1711). 2 dau

56. Marie Josephe, m. King of Saxony and Poland.
57. Marie Amelia, afterwards wife of Emperor Charles VI, 1711-1740

58. Sophia (1630-1714)

59. George Lewis (George I)

Bibliography

Anon, *The Stuarts in Italy,* Quarterly Review, Vol. 107, 1846
Baines, John, *The Jacobite Rising of 1715,* 1970
Belloc, Hilaire, *James II,* 1928
Bingham, Caroline, *Kings and Queens of Scotland,* 1976
Blaikie, W. B. editor, *Origins of the Forty-Five,* 1975
Bonaventura, Brother, *Journal of the Arrest and Escape of the Princess Sobieska,* Louvain.
Caryll MSS, British Library
Cassavetti, Eileen, *The Lion and the Lilies,* 1977
Clerk, Sir John of Penicuik, Roxburgh Club
Cowper, Lady, *Diary of,* 1715–17
Donaldson, William, *The Jacobite Song,* 1988
Durant, C. S., *Link Between Flemish Mystics and English Martyrs,* 1924
English Traveller in Rome, *Pamphlet,* 1721
Evelyn, John, *Diary,* 1685–9
Fiennes, Celia, *The journeys of,* 1685–1703
Forbin, Comte de, *Memoires,* Amsterdam, 1730
Forbes, Bishop Robert, *The Lyon in Mourning,* 1895–6
Forbes Leith, S. J., *Memoirs of Scottish Catholics,* 1909
Fothergill, Brian, *Cardinal King,* 1958
Gilbert, John T., Ed. *Clementina Sobieska,* 1894
Grew, E. and M., *The English Court in Exile, James II at St Germain,* 1911
Haile, Martin, *The Old Chevalier,* 1907
Herbert, Earls of Powis, *Misc. Papers and Family Papers,* National Library of Wales
Herbert, Earls of Powis, *Letters to J. Lewis,* Additional MS British Library
Hooke, Colonel N., *Negotiations in Scotland in 1707,* written by Himself, 1760
Kelly, Bernard, *Life of Henry Benedict Stuart,* 1899
Kenyon, John, *The Popish Plot,* 1972
Jesse, Mr, *Memoires of the Pretenders and their Adherants,*
Jones, G. H., *The Mainstream of Jacobitism,* 1954
Kroll, Maria (editor and translator), *Letters from Liselotte,* 1970
Lees-Milne, James, *The Last Stuarts,* 1983
Lenman, Bruce, *The Jacobite Risings in Britain 1698–1746,* 1980
Lewis, Lesley, *Connoisseurs and Secret Agents in 18th century Rome,* 1961
Lockhart, George of Carnwath, *Memoires concerning the Affairs of Scotland,* 1714

Madden, R. R., *History of the Penal Laws enacted against Roman Catholics,* 1847
McLynn, F. J., *The Jacobites,* 1985.
Mar, Earl of, *A Journal of his proceedings from his first arrival in Scotland,* 1717
Marshall, Rosalind, *Prince Charles Edward Stuart,* 1988
Maxwell MSS, Traquair House,
Maxwell MSS, University of Hull.
Miller, James, *Study in Kingship,* 1978
Mitchison, R. M., *History of Scotland,* 1970
Murray, John of Broughton, *"Memorials",* (edited by Fitzroy Bell), Scottish History Society, 1898
Oman, Carola, *Mary of Modena,* 1962
Ormonde, Duke of, *Letter to, Jacobite Attempt of 1719,* Scottish History Society.
Patten, Rev. R., *The History of the Late Rebellion with the Original Papers and Characters of the Principal Noblemen and Gentlemen concerned in it,* 1717
Pepys, Samuel, *Diary,* 1659–69
Sévigné, Marie, Marquise de, *Lettres de,* 1881
Shield and Laing, *The King Over the Water,* 1907
Stewart, H. C., Editor, *Exiled Stewarts in Italy,* 1717–1807
Stuarts of Traquair, MSS Family Letters, Traquair House
Tayler, H., *Jacobite Epilogue,* 1941
Tayler, A. and H., *A Jacobite Miscellany,* Roxburgh Club, 1948
Tayler, A. and H., *The Story of the Rising,* 1936
Tayler, H., *Lady Nithsdale and her Family,* 1939
Tayler, H, *The Jacobite Court at Rome in 1719,* Scottish History Society 1937
Terry, C. S, Ed. *The Chevalier de St George and the Jacobite Movement in his Favour,* 1901
Terry, L., George I, *A Constitutional King,* 1927
Vaughan, Herbert M., *The Last of the Royal Stuarts,* 1906
Vitelleschi, Marchesa Nobili, *A Court in Exile,* 1902

Index

Pages numbers in parentheses indicate illustrations